Reading Grade 8

Best Value Books

Table Of Contents

First Grade Skills   CD-3715   Printed in the United States Of America   ISBN 0-88724-433-5

Estimating Reading Ability

The following graded word lists may be used to estimate a student's reading grade level.

1. Ask the student to read each word in the list.

2. Keep count of the number of words the student reads from the list.

3. Estimate the student's ability to read materials at the same grade level as the grade level of the word list. Base your estimate upon:

23 or more   The student can probably read at this grade level without help.

18 - 22   The student can probably read at this grade level if given some help.

17 or less   The student can probably not read at this grade level even if given help.

1.	allergic	13.	neutral
2.	bountiful	14.	optimistic
3.	cancer	15.	pinhole
4.	coordinate	16.	recoil
5	deduce	17.	rivet
6.	enhance	18.	serial
7.	forfeit	19.	stanza
8.	gauze	20.	tangible
9.	hereafter	21.	transmit
10.	inflate	22.	unequal
11.	learner	23.	vantage
12.	meditate	24.	waxpaper
		25.	zenith

Ready-To-Use Ideas and Activities

The activities in this book will help children master the basic skills necessary to become competent learners. Remember as you read through the activities listed below, as you go through this book, that all children learn at their own rate. Although repetition is important, it is critical that we never lose sight of the fact that it is equally important to build children's self-esteem and self-confidence if we want them to become successful learners as well as good citizens.

Story Comprehension
During or after story discussion, there are two different types of questions that you can ask to ensure and enhance reading comprehension. The first type of question is a factual question. This type of question includes question words such as: who, what, when, where, and why. It can also include questions like How old is the character?, Where does the character live?, What time was it when....?, or any question that has a clear answer. The other type of question is an open-ended question. These questions will not have a clear answer. They are based on opinions about the story, not on facts. An open-ended question can be something like: Why do you think the character acted as he did?, How do you think the character felt about her actions or the actions of others?, What do you think the character will do next?, or What other ways could this story have ended?.

Flashcard ideas
The back of this book has removable flash cards that will be great for use for basic skill and enrichment activities. Pull the flash cards out and either cut them apart or, if you have access to a paper cutter, use that to cut the flash cards apart. The following is just one of the ways you may wish to use these flash cards.

Reproduce the bingo sheet on the opposite page in this book, making enough to have one for each student. Hand them out to the students. Take the flash cards and write the words on the chalk board. Have the students choose 24 of the words and write them in any order on the empty spaces of their bingo cards, writing only one word in each space. When all students have finished their cards, take the flash cards and make them in to a deck. Call out the words one at a time. Any student who has a word that you call out should make an "X" through the word to cross it out. The student who crosses out five words in a row first (Horizontally, vertically, or diagonally) wins the game. To extend the game you can continue playing until you a student crosses out all of the words on his bingo sheet.

Vocabulary Bingo

		FREE		

What Is Communication?

The word communicate means to share or make known. Almost every person in the world communicates with at least one other person every day of his life. In many ways it is easy to see how we communicate. In the classroom we listen to the teacher and other classmates as they talk. Talking and listening are kinds of auditory (listening) and oral (speaking) communication. We engage in auditory communication when we talk with others face-to-face, over the telephone, or as we listen to the radio. Speech is probably the most common form of communication, but it is certainly not the only form.

When we read we are taking part in another form of communication. Someone else has written a message of some sort, some information that we share when we read it. Letters, books, newspapers, and magazines are all types of written communication. Most written communication is visual, or uses the eyes. There is a form of writing that is not visual. Can you guess what it is? A blind person usually knows how to read books and other material. They use a special writing system called braille. Braille is an alphabet that uses raised dots that are punched onto a piece of paper. A person who learns the braille letters can read by feeling the raised letters as they slide their fingertips across them. This written form of communication uses the sense of touch and is called kinesthetic.

Sometimes we may watch a movie or a video in class or after school. Because the film is sharing information with us, this too is a form of communication. Movies, videos, and most filmstrips combine visual and auditory communication. You receive information through use of both your eyes and your ears. Try turning the sound off while watching a movie. It is not nearly as exciting or easy to understand when you receive only half of the intended message. Turn the sound back on, but turn your back until you cannot see the movie. Again, it is difficult to understand the full message. Television, movies, and most computers are forms of audio-visual communication that we are all familiar with.

There is another form of communication that has very little to do with words. Think about a person who is frowning and rubbing their forehead. They are communicating a message that says something is wrong, although they have not said a word. Gestures and actions are nonverbal (not oral) ways to communicate. A hug, smile, or glare sends a message that most people can understand, even if they don't speak the same language as the person sending the message.

When you think about it, there are many forms of communication. Signals are a type of communication and can be made in a variety of ways. Flashes of light, smoke, flags, drums, colors, horns, and guns have all been used to convey (send) messages. Pictures on road signs communicate warnings or other important information to travelers. Some colors and pictures have become international signals that can be recognized by people no matter what language they may speak. For example, the redcircle with a diagonal slash through it means "no" and is used in many different countries. These signals are important forms of communication that warn or help people, no matter where they are.

1. **What is the main idea of this story?**
   A. Communication is a way of sharing information and can take many forms.
   B. Signals are nonverbal forms of communication.
   C. Television and radio are the most important forms of communication.
2. **What is auditory and oral communication?**

_____

3. **Name three types of visual communication:**

_____

_____

4. **What does the word "kinesthetic" mean?**
   A. a ruler or leader
   B. running the fingertip over raised dots
   C. using the sense of touch
5. **Explain how different types of communication can be combined to give a more complete message:**

_____

_____

_____

6. **What word means "not spoken aloud"?**
   A. visual
   B. auditory
   C. nonverbal
7. **Name three types of nonverbal communication:**

_____

_____

8. **What are signals?**

_____

9. **Name five types of signals:**

_____

_____

THINK AHEAD: Draw a picture of three symbols that you find in public places. Tell what each one means.

Language

Language is a system of communication where meaningful sounds are produced and heard by the ear. Humans are the only known animals that use language. It is impossible to trace the development of language, but it is believed that humans have used it for at least the past 40,000 years. However language developed, there are somewhere between three and eight thousand different languages spoken around the world today.

Despite the fact that there are so many languages, they all share some common components, or parts. Linguists (people who study languages) agree that languages are fairly similar in organization and function. First, all languages have some form of nouns and verbs. Second, every language puts words together in groups to form sentences that express some thought. And third, every language makes a distinction among statements (I have the book.), questions (Do I have the book?), and commands (Give me the book!).

Most children from any culture learn to speak thier native language quite well by the age of four or five, even if they are not instructed. Young children also have the physical ability to pronounce sounds from other languages quite easily. This ability begins to drop off when children reach the early teen years, making it more difficult to learn a second language. Why this happens is not known, but it holds true for children of all cultures.

Language is one of the important ties that bring us all together. It allows us to express ourselves clearly as well as understand others better. We use it to gather information and to give out information. Language is a wonderful tool that we use in communicating.

1. **What is the main idea of this story?**
   A. Language is a communication tool.
   B. Different languages can be very similar, sharing common components.
   C. Humans are the only animals that use language.

2. **How did language in humans develop?**

   _____

   _____

3. **What does the word "linguist" mean?**
   A. complex structure of language
   B. ability to pronounce words at an early age
   C. a person who studies language

4. What are the three ways that all languages are similar?

_____

_____

_____

_____

5. What happens to a child's ability to learn new languages in the early teen years?

_____

_____

6. About how long has man used language?

_____

7. What are some of the important aspects of language?

_____

_____

_____

_____

_____

8. Name some ways we can communiate without speaking.

_____

_____

_____

9. What are some words or phrases you can think of from other languages?

_____

_____

_____

THINK AHEAD: Name at least three languages that are spoken by the people in your community or area.

Calls and Whistles

Perhaps you have seen a movie about early settlers in North America. These settlers could be going through a forest or sitting by a campfire at night when they hear a bird whistle, an owl hoot, or a coyote howl. They sit up, wondering if the call came from an animal or from Indians. These imitations of animal calls were often used by Indians or hunters as a means of communication.   A bird call or whistle, if done well enough, might be easily mistaken for the real thing. This allowed the hunters to keep in contact with each other and not alert the prey to the danger they were about to face.

The call of animals native to an area has been used in many parts of the world. The Comanche Indians often imitated coyotes and owls found in the areas where they lived. Some Indians along the Amazon River in South America used the call of the trumpeter bird to signal one another. Other tribes imitated the Brazilian lapwing to sound out warnings of danger. In New Guinea some of the natives would croak like frogs to signal a meeting of several villages.

These signals were very good for communicating at close distances. The wider the spread between the groups, the louder the call had to become. Groups in the Philippine Islands and India preferred to use very loud, shrill cries to communicate with each other over distances. Gomerans off the coast of Africa have developed a whistling language that can be heard from island to island, up to six miles away! Other African communities use baked clay whistles, flutes, or animal horns to send signals. By working out a code for the sounds, people are able to communicate a variety of messages over a distance that the human voice just could not reach.

1. What is the main idea of this story?
    A. Indians used bird calls to communicate while sneaking up on settlers.
    B. All kinds of animals are imitated throughout the world.
    C. Calls and whistles were used to send messages further than a voice could.

2. Why might animal calls be used even when people were close enough to shout to one another?

_____

_____

3. Name five animals that have been imitated as a form of communication:

_____

_____

_____

4. **What might the sound of a croaking frog mean in New Guinea?**

_____

_____

5. **What advantages do calls and whistles have over the human voice?**

_____

_____

6. **What kind of communication have the Gomerans developed? What is the furthest distance a message can be heard?**

_____

_____

7. **What three instruments or tools do some African tribes use to communicate with distant villages?**

_____

_____

THINK AHEAD: Describe a situation you might be in where whistles might be more helpful than words.

Drums

When we think of a drum we usually think of a musical instrument. Drums are part of almost every musical group, from small trios to huge orchestras. The drum has also been used for centuries as an important means of communication. The human voice is very good for communication, but it has one very big disadvantage: it cannot be heard very far. As early humans began to live in groups and interact with each other they needed a way to communicate with nearby villages. They could send runners from village to village with an important message, but that took a lot of time. It was discovered that beating on hollow logs could be heard for greater distances, and so a new form of communication called "talking drums" was born.

In many primitive (early) communities a large drum was set in the middle of the village to serve as a way of sending messages to nearby tribes. The drums were made of a variety of materials including goatskin, pottery, gourds, or wood. The drums ranged in size from small enough to be held by one person to eighteen feet wide or more! They could be beaten on with hands or sticks, and some produced a sound when they were rubbed. Some of the larger drums could be heard up to sixteen miles away!

The Ashanti of West Africa developed an amazing talking drum system. Their drums were made of round pieces of hollowed out wood that were four to five feet long. A skin (often an elephant ear) was stretched over one end of the wood and was held in place by a rope. The skin was tightened or loosened to produce higher and lower sounds. The Ashanti used two drums at the same time: one that made low tones (called a male) and one that made higher tones (called a female).   They had learned to use the drums so well that they could actually imitate the language that they spoke! The drums sounded much like a person speaking in a voice loud enough to be heard over a large distance.

Most systems of drum communication used a series of beats (like Morse Code) that meant something to the trained listener. The messages usually involved a notice of danger, death, war, or other news of great importance. The message could be sent great distances by a sort of relay system. That is, one village would send a message and a nearby village would hear it. They would then repeat the message on their drums, sending it on to their neighbors. Some relay systems worked so well they could send a message about 200 miles about as quickly as a telegraph could be sent!

Although "talking drums" developed into a pretty good system of communicating over distances, it had one very big disadvantage. Just as drums could be heard by the neighboring villages, they could also be heard by anyone else in the area. If approaching enemies knew how to interpret the drum messages they would know what was being said or even planned by their intended victims. Communication by drums certainly did not offer privacy!

1. **What is the main idea of this story?**
   A. The Ashanti created "talking drums".
   B. Drums have been used as a form of communication.
   C. Drums can be heard over great distances.
2. **What advantage do drums have over human voices?**

   _____

   _____

3. **What is the biggest disadvantage of using drums to communicate?**

   _____

   _____

4. **What does the word "primitive" mean?**
   A. having to do with early ages
   B. drums used as voices
   C. private
5. **What are male and female drums?**

   _____

   _____

6. **Describe a drum "relay system":**

   _____

   _____

   _____

7. **What were drums used as in primitive communities? What were they made of?**

   _____

   _____

8. **Describe an Ashanti drum.**

   _____

   _____

   _____

9. **Name 5 other forms of communication.**

   _____

   _____

   _____

THINK AHEAD: Create a communication system you could use to send messages from one place to another without using speech.

Body Language and Gestures

People do not always need to use words to communicate with others. Often their body position and gestures tell a lot more than their words do. Sending messages through positions and gestures is called body language. Body language expresses emotions and attitudes. We display how we are feeling even when our words may be saying something else. For example, a classmate tells you that she is not the least bit nervous about taking a test that day. She says she has studied hard and is confident that she will do very well. You don't really believe what she has said, but you don't know exactly why. Without either of you being aware of it, she has been sending silent messages that don't agree with what she is saying. While talking, the girl is twisting a strand of hair round and round one finger. Her eyes are darting nervously about the room and she is jiggling one foot quickly up and down. The girl's body language reveals what she is really feeling!

Researchers have found that certain acts reveal specific meanings. First, head and facial movements tell a lot about what a person is feeling. Heads that are held high send the message of pride. Twitching facial muscles may indicate extreme nervousness or anger. Second, body positions reveal how strong those feelings are. A person leaning forward in a chair is saying he is interested or sincere. Third, the eyes tell a lot about attitudes and changes in feelings. For example, avoiding direct eye contact often sends the message that the person does not feel comfortable talking in that situation. When a person is excited or interested the pupils of the eyes will dilate, or open wider.

Gestures are another form of body language that can send messages to other people. In Japan, people may greet each other with a bow to show their respect. In Tibet, a person may show respect by sticking out his tongue! Many people clap to show that they appreciate something they have just witnessed. In many cultures people also clap as a way of saying "Thank you". In China you may be regarded as disrespectful if you hand something to another person using only one hand. The object should be handed over with two hands, not one. Hugging, kissing, or pinching cheeks are common forms of greeting in some cultures. In other places these greetings are considered offensive and disrespectful.

Understanding body language and the meaning of gestures can be a full time job! There have been many books written on these topics because it is interesting and can even be helpful. Some employers are trained to become aware of body language to help them learn more about the attitudes of the people they interview for jobs. Politicians and actors are very aware of their body language because it really affects their image in public. Lawyers may use knowledge of body language to help their clients send the appropriate message to the jury. What does your body language say about you?

1. **What is the main idea of this story?**
   A. Body language and gestures can send messages that are stronger than words.
   B. Body language is different all over the world.
   C. Body language and gestures are not forms of communication.

2. **What is body language?**

   _____

   _____

3. **Are most people aware of body language? Explain why or why not.**

   _____

   _____

4. **What movements tell a lot about what a person is feeling?**

   _____

   _____

5. **What do body positions tell about a person?**

   _____

   _____

6. **When a person will not look you in the eye when you are talking, what does that mean?**

   _____

   _____

7. **What word means "to open wider"?**
   A. body language
   B. twitching
   C. dilate

8. **What is the difference between body language and gestures?**

   _____

   _____

9. **What is one way of showing that you appreciate something you have just witnessed?**

   _____

   _____

THINK AHEAD: Make a list of eight gestures that have a specific meaning in your culture.

Pictures

Long before man could write he was painting pictures to communicate messages. Pictures carved on the walls of caves have been found throughout the world and can date back 15 to 25 thousand years. Many of these pictures were found deep in caves where there is no light. The artist had to paint by the light of burning moss or melted fat. We know that because a lot of these "lamps" have been found in the caves near the paintings. Each of these pictures tells a story of life long ago. They are still sending messages thousands of years after they were drawn!

Paintings were created by smearing the color on with fingers or a brush. They were usually done in only one or two colors (mainly using yellow, red, black, brown, or white). The Bushmen of Africa were very busy artists. They painted pictures that depict (or describe) animals, hunting methods, weapons, household items, customs, ceremonies, and warfare. The Bushmen used a wide variety of colors - red, orange, yellow, black, and white were most commonly used. Paintings such as these help us trace history and see how people used to live.

Most primitive art was not made by painting. More often the picture was made by etching, or carving, the stone. These ancient carvings are called petroglyphs (Greek for rock carving). Petroglyphs have been found on every continent! They were produced in many different ways. Some petroglyphs were made by rubbing or scratching with a hard stone or tool. Others were chiseled, using a small sharp stone and hitting it with a bigger stone. If you have ever tried to carve your initials on a stone you will know that making petroglyphs was not an easy task!

Pictures are more likely to be found in caves where they are protected from the weather. Petroglyphs, on the other hand, can be found almost any place where there is smooth rock. They can be found all over North and South America, Africa, Australia, and parts of Europe and Asia. You will not find many petroglyphs in the jungles, because most of the rocks there are covered with plants which makes it difficult to find a spot on which to carve.

Many areas where paintings or petroglyphs have been found were made into national monuments or taken to museums in an effort to preserve, or save, them. Many books and magazine articles have discussed these drawings and presented ideas as to what they mean. However, scientists and archaeologists can only guess at their true meaning.   It is believed that many of the pictures were connected with religious groups or certain ceremonial rituals. Other pictures may have simply been a way to record important events in the lives of the people who drew them.

The art of cave drawing and rock carving may seem primitive but some modern art is still exhibited in the same way. Graffiti is common on the walls in most major cities and can also be found in rocky areas. Our methods of creating the paintings have changed (we often use spray paint or metal tools) but the purpose is still a means of expression. What will the scientists of the future think when they uncover our petroglyphs and "wall paintings" ?

1. **What is the main idea of this story?**
    A. Ancient cave drawings can be found throughout the world.
    B. Petroglyphs are rock carvings.
    C.The practice of drawing messages or stories in public places is thousands of years old.

2. **How did ancient cave artists provide light so they could see in these dark places?**

_____

_____

3. **What were the most common colors used in cave painting?**

_____

_____

4. **What does the word "depict" mean?**
    A. rock carving
    B. represent or describe
    C. early descriptions of hunting

5. **What is the difference between a painting and a petroglyph?**

_____

_____

6. **Which word means "to save or keep safe"?**
    A. petroglyph
    B. etching
    C. preserve

7. **What do scientists believe most of this ancient art was used for?**

_____

_____

THINK AHEAD: What forms of modern "cave art" have you seen? What do you think it meant?

14   CD-3715

Writing

Writing is a relatively new invention, dating back only 5,000 years or so. It is not known who invented writing, or exactly when it was created. Scientists do believe that it developed somewhere in Mesopotamia, the land between the Tigris and Euphrates Rivers (what we now call Iraq). The reason we believe this is because archaeologists found clay tablets there, the earliest example of writing ever to be discovered. People called Sumerians lived in that area 5,000 years ago. They were highly civilized, living in cities with temples, businesses, and even banks. The Sumerians developed a sense of personal property, things belonging to an individual instead of a group. It became important to identify who owned which animals, tools, and land. At this time people began to mark their belongings with a personal picture or symbol. They often put their mark on a stone cylinder which they could press into a piece of soft clay or wax. This was the first time pictures began to stand for words.

This stage of development was fairly easy at first. A picture of a cow could represent a cow, a sheep stood for a sheep, and so on. Pictures were good for concrete, or real thing, but pictures could not represent ideas such as sorrow, old, or eat. The Sumerians began to combine pictures to try to represent ideas. For example, an eye with tears falling from it might be used to stand for sorrow. Combining pictures to represent ideas is called ideographs. This was the second stage in writing. The biggest problem with ideographs was that pictures might be interpreted differently by different people. The limits of this system pushed the development to a third, a very important, stage.

The Sumerians realized that ideographs could be used to represent sounds as well as objects. A modern example would be a picture of a bee and a leaf. The two pictures as objects mean very little, but the sounds put together give us the word belief. This was the beginning of writing based on phonics, or sounds. Over the years the pictures were changed into marks that were easier to write. These marks were eventually developed into alphabets, symbols representing the smallest unit of meaningful sound. Records and messages could now be written, no matter what idea the writer wanted to express.

Clay was plentiful in Mesopotamia. It could be scooped up almost anywhere along the riverbanks. Clay could also be flattened out and smoothed, making it an excellent place to write. The Sumerians used these clay writing tablets for the next two or three thousand years! The earliest tablets show that the scribes, or people who could write, recorded information in vertical columns beginning at the upper right corner. They wrote down the column to the bottom of the tablet then moved left and back to the top. This system was not used for long, however. Perhaps the scribes became frustrated with having their hand smudge the words as they moved to the left column. Think about writing from right to left: your hand drags over the words you have just written. At any rate, before long it became the custom to begin at the top left and write across the tablet, as most people do today.

1. **What is the main idea of this story?**
   A. Writing was developed in Mesopotamia about 5,000 years ago.
   B. Writing began with pictures representing objects.
   C. The Sumerians were highly civilized people.

2. **Where is the land that was once called Mesopotamia?**

   _____

   _____

3. **Why did the Sumerians have a need for writing?**

   _____

   _____

4. **What does the word "concrete" mean as it is used in the story?**
   A. a hard stone-like material
   B. real or able to be touched
   C. the smallest unit of meaningful sound

5. **What symbols were used during the second stage of writing development?**

   _____

   _____

6. **What does the word "phonics" mean?**
   A. alphabetical
   B. ideographs
   C. the smallest unit of sound

7. **What were scribes?**

   _____

   _____

8. **What was so important about representing sounds rather than objects?**

   _____

   _____

THINK AHEAD: Think of at least three examples of words that can be written ideographically. Draw them in picture form.

Sign Language

Speaking and writing are wonderful ways to communicate. What happens, however, when two people who speak different languages try to talk with each other? How can the deaf communicate if they cannot hear what is being said? Sign language is a way of communicating without voices that can be used in a variety of situations.

The most widely used sign languages are those used by the deaf. For hundreds of years people who could not hear have used gestures to express themselves. In the mid 1700's a man in France began the first school for the deaf. The common signs used by these people became the basis for an entire non-verbal language system. The signs represent letters, words, or word groups that are put into the sentence structure of the verbal language being signed.

A different form of signing was developed by the Plains Indians so they could communicate with tribes that spoke other languages. Gestures were developed to represent a small vocabulary important to those tribes. Signs for complex ideas were not needed because the Indians had a fairly common background and could also use their verbal language.

1. **What is the main idea of this story?**
    A. Sign language is a nonverbal way to communicate.
    B. Sign language is difficult to learn.
    C. The Plains Indians developed a simple sign language.
2. **What contributed to the need for developing a sign language?**

_____

_____

3. **Who developed the most commonly used sign language?**

_____

4. **What three parts of language can signs represent?**

_____

5. **Which Indians developed a form of sign language?**

_____

6. **Why wasn't Indian sign language as complex as sign language for the deaf?**

_____

_____

THINK AHEAD: In what other ways is sign language used? (Hint: Think of sports!)

Braille

For hundreds of years people who were blind or had poor vision had no way to read. They had to rely on verbal communication for most of their learning experiences. In 1829 a man named Louis Braille invented a new system of communication for the blind. He developed an alphabet, numbers, and punctuation marks made up of dots. Different combinations using one to six dots represented different letters, numbers, or letter groups. These dots were pressed into a piece of paper or other flat surface. By lightly running the tips of the fingers across the dots a person was able to read with their hands.

Braille was not widely accepted at first, but by 1932 a standard Braille system for people who spoke English had been instituted, or established, and was used in many schools. Books printed in Braille were now available to people with visual problems. For a number of years Braille has been taught in schools for the blind and visually impaired.

Today tape recorders and computers have made it easier for blind people to learn. There are even machines that can translate (change) the spoken word into print. A visually impaired person can write a letter simply by speaking to the computer! This new technology has created some new problems, however. Blind people who have not learned Braille are finding it very difficult to get good jobs without this skill. It is comparable to a sighted person not being able to read. Use of the television or verbal computer programs is not enough to function at work on an affective level. A few states have laws requiring that Braille be taught to all blind people that are capable of learning it.

1. **What is the main idea of this story?**
    A. Braille is an important means of communication for people with visual impairments.
    B. Braille is a system of dots that can be read with the fingertips.
    C. Louis Braille invented Braille in 1829.
2. **What is Braille?**

    _____

    _____

    _____

3. **How do the blind use their hands when reading Braille?**

    _____

    _____

4. Where was Braille commonly taught after 1932?

_____

5. What does the word "translate" mean?
    A. to type Braille
    B. to change from one language to another
    C. to read Braille

6. What has caused people to stop using Braille?

_____

_____

7. Why is it important for the blind to learn Braille?

_____

_____

8. What did blind people rely on for most of their learning experiences before Braille was developed?

_____

9. What are some modern ways that blind people learn other than by reading Braille?

_____

_____

THINK AHEAD: Write a short paragraph describing how your life would be changed if you were suddenly blind. Do you think you would try to learn Braille? Why or why not?

Telegraph

For most of the history of man, communication could be transmitted (sent) in two ways: sight and sound. Sight signals were sent by things such as fires, smoke, or light. Bells, whistles, drums, and the human voice were common forms of communication by sound. During the early 1800's, the world was growing rapidly and the need for a fast system of long distance communication was in demand. The discovery of controlled electricity opened the door to that kind of system.

The world was beginning to work with electricity and began to understand it a little better. People quickly realized that it had great power and were interested in finding ways to use it. When it was discovered that electricity could travel over great distances through a tiny wire it was only natural that scientists and inventors thought to apply it to long distance communication. Many people experimented with the idea, so it is not surprising that the first telegraph was not a quick invention thought up by one man. Rather, it was the result of a series of experiments by a number of men, each making a little more progress than the last.

The early telegraph was a very simple machine. It was discovered that an electrical current could be sent through a wire for great distances. It was discovered that when a switch or a key was connected to one end, a person could send a series of short pulses through the wire. The only problem was that no one had figured out a way to receive the pulses at the other end of the line. This problem was solved in 1819 when Hans Oersted discovered that a magnetic needle would react to the electrified wire. These telegraphs became known as electric telegraphs.

In 1831 Samuel Morse devised, or invented, a receiver that would produce a clicking sound when attached to an electric wire. Morse also invented a coding system of dots and dashes that worked really well with the clicking receiver. In 1844 Morse demonstrated this new telegraph by successfully sending a message from Baltimore, Maryland to Washington, D.C. for a group of politicians. Morse's receiver became very popular and was widely adopted. The coding system was easy to learn and could be plainly understood on the clicking telegraph. The system was named after Samuel Morse (Morse Code) and is still used in some situations today.

1. **What is the main idea of this story?**
   A. Samuel Morse invented the electric telegraph.
   B. Early telegraphs were simple machines.
   C. The telegraph is a way to communicate using electricity and a code of dots and dashes.
2. **Before electricity was used, what were the only two ways to send messages?**

_____

_____

3. How did the discovery of electricity affect our systems of communication?

_____

_____

4. What was the problem with early telegraph machines?

_____

_____

5. What did Hans Oersted discover in 1819?

_____

_____

6. What does the word "transmit" mean?
   A. to invent
   B. to click out in code
   C. to send

7. What was used as the first receiver for the telegraph?

_____

_____

8. Who invented a "clicking" receiver and a communication coding system?

_____

_____

9. What word means "to invent"?
   A. transmit
   B. devise
   C. code

10. Why did Morse Code become accepted so quickly?

_____

_____

THINK AHEAD: Find out more about Morse Code by looking in the encyclopedia or other reference book. Write a short message using Morse Code.

Telephone

In 1875 Alexander Graham Bell was very interested in the communication problems of the hearing impaired. Bell taught in a school for the deaf, intent on teaching the students how to speak clearly enough to be understood. Because of this interest, Bell invented a machine, the phonautograph, that could record the human voice. Deaf students would speak into this machine as a pencil recorded their speech on a piece of paper. Bell believed that the deaf students could compare the penciled speech patterns with normal speech patterns and correct themselves. His work was successful enough to gain nationwide attention.

Other people who saw Bell's phonautograph saw its potential as a communication device, a way to send the human voice. They encouraged Bell to experiment with the machine, but he was not sure because he knew nothing about electricity. Bell got an assistant, Thomas Watson, who had worked quite a bit with electrical inventions. Bell and Watson tried many experiments with transmitters and receivers and on March 10, 1876 they finally found a way to make the first telephone work.

The telephone was first used in several Boston banks as security systems. The transmitters were installed in the banks and left on all night while a private detective agency listened for intruders. The idea caught on and before long businessmen began to use the telephone as a quick means of communicating among themselves. Within one year of its discovery, the telephone system had been successfully used in Boston and New Haven. Although these systems were fairly small, Bell was ready to open his invention to the world.

By 1888 the telephone had become commonplace in the businesses of large cities. Wires were strung on poles and could be seen throughout the cities and crossing the countryside between cities. The wires created new problems. It took many wires to service the demand for telephones. Soon the poles were thick with telephone lines. During a fire, firemen often had to cut through wires to reach the buildings with their ladders. Heavy snow or ice storms usually snapped wires and caused problems with communications. The problem of hanging wires was eventually solved when they were bundled into cables and buried underground.

As the telephone became common in more and more homes, the system went through many changes as it struggled to keep up with the increase of users. It was clear that even the heavy underground cables could not supply enough circuits to meet the demand. Because all calls had to go through an operator, the telephone exchange companies rapidly grew, but they still could not keep up with the number of calls to be handled. People enjoyed the advantages of having a telephone, and they wanted the service to be faster and easier.

Bell's little business had expanded into a huge company. Its engineers experimented with different ways to improve the system and solve new problems. The dial was invented, allowing customers to call someone directly and not have to speak with an operator. The dial has rapidly given way to push button telephones, an even faster way to "dial" a number. The heavy underground cables have been replaced with flexible glass tubes able to carry many times more circuits than the old wires. Telephones are in nearly every home in North America. Thanks to the invention of portable phones, we can even take them with us when we leave the house! Bell's simple invention to help deaf children has evolved into one of the most important communication systems in the world today.

1. **What is the main idea of this story?**
   A. Alexander Graham Bell taught deaf children.
   B. The telephone has become a very important communication tool.
   C. Early telephones created many new problems for cities.

2. **Why did Bell become interested in recording the human voice?**

   _____

   _____

3. **What was the "phonautograph"?**
   A. an autograph given by telephone
   B. the first phonograph
   C. a machine that could record voices

4. **Why did Bell choose Thomas Watson as his assistant?**

   _____

   _____

5. **In what uncommon way did the Boston banks first use the telephone?**

   _____

   _____

6. **What problems did telephone wires create?**

   _____

   _____

7. **How did the invention of the telephone dial improve communication?**

   _____

   _____

THINK AHEAD: Keep a record of telephone calls for one day. Keep track of the number of local and long distance calls. How many calls are for business? For pleasure? How many different ways is your phone used to communicate?

What is Conservation?

What happens when you use your last sheet of paper? You, of course, go to the store and buy some more. Pretend that the pack of paper you buy is the last one in the world. Would you waste sheets carelessly, or would you use them only when necessary? What would you do when you ran out again? This may seem like a silly problem because we are talking about plain old paper, but did you know that paper is made from trees? We rely on trees for many other important things such as producing food, providing shade, and even cleaning the air we breathe. If the world ran out of paper it would probably be because there were only enough trees left to provide the more important things we need. The world is not running out of paper, so don't get upset yet, but this problem could happen one day.

During the history of man the earth has seemed like a huge place that was full of resources, or available natural materials. The world population was not very big and the earth was able to produce more materials than man could use. People did not think twice about digging holes to look for gold or chopping down trees to build homes. The supply of natural resources was vast, seeming to have no end. The discovery of two new continents in the 1700's reinforced (supported) the idea of endlessness. These continents were huge land masses full of furs, trees, ore, and other materials people wanted. Few people imagined that the land would ever run out of anything!

During the 1800's the need for lumber was important as the world population increased and many new cities were built. North America was covered with large forests and was a rich source for much of the needed wood. Logging became a booming business with many acres being cleared each day. Forests that had taken hundreds of years to grow were gone within a few years. People began to realize that it would take hundreds of years to replace these forests and, for the first time, they began to worry. Was it possible that man could "use up" the natural resources?

By the late 1800's groups began to organize and plan ways to conserve, or use wisely, our natural resources. They realized that everything on the earth has a limit, and that wasting resources could bring us to the end very quickly. Humans could not stop using wood, for example, but they could control how much was used and what was being done to replace it for the future. Rules and laws were made about the use of forests, soil, and certain wildlife. The world came to understand that we must take care of the earth if we expected the earth to provide for our future needs.

Today, conservation is more than a plan to save trees or animals. It has become a management system for the total environment (everything around us). Scientists have discovered how nature is interrelated, or how each living thing relies on other living things for its survival. Every plant and animal has a purpose and if it is taken away, the absence affects everything else in one way or another. For example, no one is very fond of mosquitoes. At times, almost everyone has wished that there were no mosquitoes! What would happen if they were all destroyed? We might be happy for a while, but soon we would notice a big change. Many small animals that eat mosquitoes, like birds and frogs, would starve. The larger animals that fed on these smaller animals would have less food and would begin to die out. Before long even man would feel the affects by having less available food for himself.

Today, conservationists consider everything in nature and weigh it against the needs of people. We need to use materials from the earth, but we cannot afford to waste them. We are now worried about how things like water and air are used because we realize that the supply is not unlimited. Conservation serves as a balance between what we have to use and what we should not use.

1. What is the main idea of this story?
    A. Conservation of natural resources is important to the future survival of humans.
    B. Loggers cut down too many trees and wasted lumber.
    C. Everything on the earth is important.

2. Why did people once believe that resources were unlimited?

_____

_____

3. When did people really begin to realize that there was a need to conserve our natural resources?

_____

_____

4. What does the word "reinforce" mean?
    A. conserve natural resources
    B. strengthen or support
    C. everything around us

5. Why is every part of the environment important to our survival?

_____

_____

6. How can the conservation of today help people in the future?

_____

_____

THINK AHEAD: List four resources (animals or materials) that are being wasted or destroyed. How might the loss of these resources affect you?

Soil Erosion

"That thing is as useless as dirt!" This saying tells a lot about what we think of dirt. We walk on it and dig in it, but we don't really use it for anything important, do we? Think again. Soil is very important to the survival of humans. We grow plants in soil. We find necessary minerals in soil. It truly is an important resource that we must protect. You might ask, "How in the world can you misuse soil?" This is a good question and here is a good answer.

Dirt is full of minerals that are necessary to grow plants. Farmers have learned that adding minerals to the dirt can help produce healthier crops. They have also learned that you cannot grow the same crop in the same field year after year. For example, a crop like corn requires specific minerals to grow. Each year corn is planted, the crop uses more of that mineral. After two or three years that mineral is no longer plentiful and the corn plants begin to suffer. Agricultural (farming) specialists have discovered that crops should be rotated, or changed, from year to year. Planting a crop that requires a different mineral allows the soil to replenish, or restock, the minerals that were used the year before.

Some forms of mining can also hurt the soil. Coal was once a very important source of power. As the demand for coal grew, many mines were established. Tunneling into the earth took a long time and was dangerous work. Coal could not be dug out fast enough to supply the demand. Someone discovered that when coal deposits were fairly close to the surface of the earth it was possible to "strip" the earth away without tunneling (sort of like peeling an orange). Strip mining became very common, tearing up thousands of acres of land each year. When the coal had been mined the stripped land was useless for growing crops.

Erosion, or gradually wearing away, is another problem for soil. Wind blows across the land, often lifting bits of topsoil and carrying it away. Heavy rains and floods flow over the land, pushing and carrying loose soil with it. Wind and water are the two biggest causes of soil erosion. How can we stop the wind from blowing or the rain from falling? We cannot, of course, but we can stop the soil from eroding. Agricultural specialists have found that plants help to keep soil where it belongs. Rows of trees planted around a field help to break the wind so it doesn't carry off the rich topsoil. Proper irrigation (watering) and draining of fields can help to keep water from carrying away large amounts of soil.

Soil is an important resource that we must protect if we want to keep growing food. Now, if you ever hear someone use the expression, "it is as useless as dirt", you will be able to tell them that dirt is far from useless!

1. **What is the main idea of this story?**
    A. Soil is an important natural resource that needs to be properly conserved.
    B. The saying "useless as dirt" is not true.
    C. Strip mining and crops are harmful to the topsoil.
2. **Another word for agricultural is:**
    A. peeling
    B. farming
    C. tunneling
3. **Why is soil an important resource?**

    _____

    _____

4. **Why should crops be rotated every two or three years?**

    _____

    _____

5. **What is strip mining?**

    _____

    _____

6. **What does the word "replenish" mean?**
    A. to remove the upper layer of soil
    B. to refill or restock
    C. to gradually wear away
7. **What are the two biggest causes of soil erosion?**

    _____

    _____

8. **What can people do to prevent soil erosion?**

    _____

    _____

THINK AHEAD: Look up the Dust Bowl in the encyclopedia. What did it have to do with soil erosion?

Land

The world's population is increasing at a rapid rate. More people means that we need more land to grow the crops that supply food. At the same time, more people means a need for more land to live on. Some scientists believe that the world population will eventually be much larger than our food production and widespread famine (food shortage) will occur. Other authorities believe that we can prevent this from happening if appropriate government policies, research, and technology are used.

Agriculture depends on arable land (land that is suitable for growing crops). The world has about three billion acres of arable land. Currently, less than half of it is being used for farming and we lose millions of acres of it each year. There are several reasons that this arable land is not in use, or disappearing. First, much of this arable land is not ready for production. The largest areas of unused arable land are in Africa. Huge amounts of money will be needed to clear the land, level it, put in irrigation systems, and control for diseases. Second, about 2.5 million acres are lost each year because of improper land management. Much of the arable land is being deforested (cut for timber) or overgrazed by animals. The loss of vegetation, or plant cover is causing erosion. There is a possibility that the land could become desert before it can be saved. Third, about 1.5 million acres of arable land is lost each year as new homes and businesses are built on it.

1. **What is the main idea of this story?**
   A. The world is losing millions of acres of arable land each year.
   B. Countries are trying to save their land for farming.
   C. Much of our land is eroding and turning into desert.
2. **Why do some scientists predict a famine in the future?**

   _____

   _____

3. **What does the word "arable" mean?**
   A. deforested
   B. covered with plants
   C. suitable for farming
4. **Name two reasons that we lose so much arable land each year.**

   _____

   _____

THINK AHEAD: Outline a plan to provide housing for the growing world population without using any more of the arable land.

Rain Forests

Tropical rainforests (also known as jungles) grow in warm wet regions and can be found in Central and South America, Africa, and Southeast Asia. They are called rainforests because of the heavy amount of rain that falls year round (80 to 160 inches annually). Because it has a warm moist climate, the rainforest is a kind of "hothouse" where plants can grow all year long. Rainforests are thick with vegetation, supporting more than half of all known types of plants in the world. The variety of vegetation helps to support thousands of animal species. For example, a scientist exploring just 2.5 acres of rainforest will find over 200 kinds of trees and plants!

Rainforests are dark and mysterious places that have not been fully explored. They take up less than eight percent of the earth, but more than half of all plant and animal species live there. The thick growth makes it difficult to get very far into the jungle. Most exploration must be done on foot or, in some areas, by boat. Large portions of the rainforests have not been explored yet. It is believed that there are many plants and animals in these areas that have not yet been discovered!

Rainforests also support over half of the known animal species of the world. Recently a scientist conducted research in the rainforests of Panama and Peru. He has estimated that there may be over 30 million species of insects alone in the rainforests! You can also find most reptile, amphibian, and tree dwelling species of animals living within a rainforest. The variety of animals found there number in the thousands.

Tropical rainforests are a rich source of food, medicine, and other useful products. Chocolate, banana, pineapple, and avocado are a few of the foods that originated in these jungles. One out of every four drug prescriptions we use are made from plants that grow in rainforests. Scientists believe that the remedy for such diseases as cancer and heart disease may be found in the plants that grow in the jungle. Many of the plants from the rainforest supply us with products that are a part of our daily lives including chicle (the base for gum), rubber, and cinnamon.

The rainforests are important to the world in many ways. Some of the undiscovered plants and animals may hold the answer to problems of hunger and disease that some of the world now faces. It is impossible to know for certain until the rainforests have been fully explored. One thing we do know at this time is that rainforests are an important part of the world ecology (balance of nature). However, about 30,000 square miles of rainforest are burned or cut down each year. The land is then used for ranching, farming, or industry. It is estimated that 1,000 species of plants and animals are eradicated, or become extinct, each year due to the loss of rainforests. Five out of six species that are destroyed have never been seen by scientists!

Many people understand the importance of preserving, or saving, the rainforests. There are several groups that are active in trying to stop the destruction of these valuable resources. National parks and reserves can be found in most tropical areas. Local farmers are being taught how to produce crops without destroying the rainforest. Through these efforts, perhaps we can save the rainforests which give us so much.

1. **What is the main idea of this story?**
    a. Chewing gum is made from a tropical plant.
    b. Rainforests are being destroyed.
    c. Rainforests are an important part of the world ecological system.

2. **Why are rainforests a great place for plants to grow?**

_____

_____

3. **How many types of trees can typically be found in a 2.5 acre jungle?**

_____

4. **Name four products we use that come from the rainforest:**

_____

_____

5. **What does the word "eradicate" mean?**
    a. to wipe out or destroy
    b. to cut down or burn
    c. to save

6. **Why are scientists concerned about losing so many acres of rainforest each year?**

_____

_____

7. **What word means "to save from destruction"?**
    a. ecology
    b. eradicate
    c. preserve

THINK AHEAD: What might happen to the world if deforesting is allowed to continue?

Water

Water is one of our most important natural resources. It is essential (necessary) to all living things. At first glance, the earth's water sources seem limitless. Two-thirds of our planet is covered with water. The oceans and seas contain salt water while lakes, rivers, and ponds contain fresh water. It is used for transportation, irrigation, and recreation. Water also supplies much of our sources of food and energy. Dams are built on rivers to supply power for electricity and reservoirs, or water storage areas, for recreation and wildlife.

Using the water to satisfy human needs is necessary and a good thing. Unfortunately, many ways in which we use the water create waste products, or pollution, that can poison our water supply. Four major causes of water pollution are human waste, factory waste, farm byproducts, and dumping trash.

For many years water has been used as a place to dump unwanted materials. City sewerage systems often got rid of untreated human waste by draining it into nearby water supplies. Although rules and laws were made to stop this from happening, it continues to be a problem in many parts of the world.

Factories produce many products that are necessary to our everyday lives. However, they also produce waste products that must be removed. For many years factories found that the easiest and cheapest way to get rid of their waste was to dump it into rivers and seas. They thought the waste would disappear, or be absorbed back into the water, dirt, or air. We now know that most waste products are not absorbed and do not disappear at all. Instead, they remain in the water and create a danger for animals and humans.

Farmers lose part of their crops to insect pests every year. One way to control this is to spray the crops with chemicals called pesticides. These chemicals kill the insects that destroy their crops and are very helpful in keeping our food supply stable. However, these chemicals do not disappear once they have done their job. They are usually washed into the soil by rain and can find their way into groundwater supplies (pools of water under the soil) that are used as drinking water for nearby towns and cities. Drinking water supplies must now be treated for chemicals such as these pesticides before the water can be piped to homes and businesses.

Each day large cities produce tons of rubbish and trash. One solution to getting rid of trash is to bury it in places called dumps. It has been discovered that chemicals and liquid from this rotting trash can leak into the surrounding groundwater, much as the pesticides do. A second solution commonly used today is to load the trash on barges and dump it into the ocean far off shore. We know that the ocean will not dissolve and absorb the trash, but many people argue that the ocean is very big and a little trash will not seriously harm it.

As more and more of our "unlimited" water supply becomes polluted, people are doing things to help. Laws have been passed to prevent dumping all waste products in or near our water supplies and oceans. Many countries are launching projects aimed at cleaning up polluted rivers and lakes. Others are trying to make everyone aware that we do have a problem and it is time to do something about it.

1. **What is the main idea of this story?**
    A. Cities are dumping waste into the water.
    B. Factories are a major cause of water pollution.
    C. Water pollution has become a big problem.
2. **What are some of the ways we use water?**

_____

_____

3. **What is pollution?**

_____

_____

4. **Name the four major causes of water pollution discussed in this article:**

_____

_____

5. **What does the word "pesticide" mean?**
    A. a chemical used to kill insect pests
    B. a form of pollution
    C. absorption of chemicals into the soil
6. **In what two ways do people usually get rid of trash or rubbish?**

_____

_____

7. **What did people believe would happen to the waste dumped into rivers?**

_____

_____

8. **What things are people doing to prevent water pollution?**

_____

_____

THINK AHEAD: What does your community do to prevent water pollution?

Smog

Nothing is more essential to human life than the air we breathe. Without air, a person will die within minutes. Despite this fact, the very air we breathe is constantly being polluted. Many of the things that help us live more comfortably are major causes of air pollution - power and heat generators, burning solid wastes, industries, and transportation. Small particles of waste turned loose in the air help create dirty clouds commonly known as smog, which has affected more people than any other type of air pollution.

Smog usually occurs in cities where the concentration of air pollution is higher than in rural areas. Smoke in the air provides particles on which water vapor will condense, creating a combination of smoke and fog. Smog can become so thick it actually reduces visibility (how far you can see) and can cause many kinds of respiratory problems. It has also been known to produce eye irritation and can damage many types of plants. In 1952, the smog in London was so thick it is believed to have causes about 4,000 deaths.

Although factories and airplanes are major causes of air pollution, individual people are a part of the problem as well. Each person who drives a vehicle to work or school each day contributes to the dangerous gases in the air. Widespread use of aerosol cans (spray cans using fluorocarbons) releases chemicals that reduce the ozone layer, a gas which helps protect the earth's atmosphere. Burning leaves or rubbish puts many pollutants into the air and contribute to the problem.

Some things are being done to help reduce the amount of smog. Special devices have been added to motor vehicles to reduce the amount of dangerous gases they produce. Laws have been passed to force industries to reduce the amount of pollutants they produce. Gasoline companies have stopped adding lead to their product, reducing the pollution it causes. Some cities have banned burning leaves and rubbish at any time. Other cities do not allow fires in stoves or fireplaces except on days when the wind is strong enough to carry the smoke away from the city. Aerosol cans have been replaced with pump sprays to reduce the use of fluorocarbons. Many individuals have formed car pools where groups of people ride to work or school together rather than each person taking his own vehicle.

The cost of cleaning up the air after it has been polluted is very high. Some methods of cleaning the air actually produce other forms of pollution that must be dealt with. Air pollution is certainly not an easy problem to solve! Although we have a long way to go before our air is clean again, many people are constantly working on new solutions to this big problem.

1. **What is the main idea of this story?**
   A. Many people in London died because of smog.
   B. Air pollution, and smog in particular, has created many health problems.
   C. Air is necessary to all living things.

2. **What are some of the causes of pollution?**

   _____

   _____

3. **What is smog?**

   _____

   _____

4. **What are some problems caused by smog?**

   _____

   _____

5. **What word means "ability to see at a distance"?**
   A. smog
   B. visibility
   C. pollutant

6. **Name three things that contribute to smog:**

   _____

   _____

7. **What is an "aerosol can"?**

   _____

   _____

8. **What is being done to reduce smog produced by vehicles?**

   _____

   _____

9. **How can individuals help reduce the amount of air pollution?**

   _____

   _____

10. **Why is it so difficult to clean polluted air?**

    _____

    _____

    _____

THINK AHEAD: What can you do to help fight air pollution?

34   CD-3715

Acid Rain

Acid rain is a type of pollution that is creating many problems for the air, land, and water. Acid rain is formed when water vapor in the air condenses on sulfur and nitrogen dioxides. This acid filled water may sit over the land as a fog or it can fall as rain, snow, or hail. Acid rain has destroyed lakes containing plant and animal life, caused damage to forests and crops, and contaminated drinking water. Winds often carry these clouds great distances before the acid rain finally falls. The damaging affects of acid rain have been found in Europe, North America, and Africa.

Sulfur in the air comes mainly from the burning of oil or coal. Some factories that use these fuels are required to install expensive air cleaners called scrubbers in their smokestacks to reduce the amount of sulfur they release into the air. Other factories have begun to use coal with a lower sulfur content. Nitrogen oxides are generally produced from automobile engines. More people than ever own one or two cars so the problem has grown considerably in the past few years. Car manufacturers are now required to use devices that help reduce the amount of this dangerous gas.

1. **What is the main idea of this story?**
    A. Cars contribute to the formation of acid rain.
    B. Acid rain can be found in many parts of the world.
    C. Acid rain pollutes air, land, and water.

2. **What is acid rain?**

    _____

    _____

3. **What are the damaging effects of acid rain?**

    _____

    _____

4. **What are "scrubbers"?**
    A. devices that remove sulfur from the air
    B. devices put on cars to remove nitrogen oxides
    C. contaminated drinking water

5. **What is the biggest producer of nitrogen oxide?**

    _____

    _____

THINK AHEAD: Find out more about acid rain. What can be done to control this problem?

Recycling

In the past, materials used as containers or wraps were considered waste. They were burned, buried, or dumped into the ocean when they were no longer useful. Today people are more concerned with how our trash is being disposed of, or gotten rid of. We realize that trash cannot be burned because it releases harmful gases into the air. It cannot be buried because much of it never decomposes, or turns back into natural elements. (Plastic, for example, will remain in the same form for thousands of years!) Buried trash can also create chemicals that contaminate underground water supplies. Dumping trash into the ocean may seem like a quick solution, but we all know that this practice cannot continue or we will ruin the oceans, too.

Recycling is a very practical way of handling our trash. Some metals, paper, glass, and plastic can be recycled, or processed and used again. For example, a glass or plastic beverage container that is discarded will never decompose or melt down, but that is only half of the problem. A new bottle must be made to replace the one that was discarded. Materials that produce glass or plastic must be purchased and processed to produce the new bottle. If the bottle is recycled rather than discarded, it does not create waste or cost a lot to prepare for reuse.

Recycling products is a good control for pollution, but it is not without problems of its own. One problem is the separation of types of trash. Metal, paper, glass, and plastic cannot all be treated the same way if it is to be reused. Recycling programs in cities require people to separate their trash in groups of paper, glass, metal, plastic, and garbage (food waste). This process helps the recyclers in the sorting process, but separating trash is not as easy as it appears. People are not happy about having to set out five cans instead of the usual one garbage can.

New methods for separating the materials have been developed. Now people only need to separate the garbage from the trash. The garbage is hauled away and disposed of. Trash is taken to a processing plant where the lighter material (paper) is taken out. The paper is either burned to produce power or shredded and reformed as cardboard, paper bags, newsprint, and other paper products. The rest of the trash is put on a conveyor belt and sent down a line. The belt passes by electromagnet and other devices that separate the trash into groups of metal, plastic, and glass. The metals are sold as scrap to be melted down and reused. Plastics may be melted and reused or shredded for use as fiberfill. Glass is separated by color then melted and reused.

The energy used to reprocess waste materials is usually much less than it takes to make the same product from all new materials. Recycling, however, can end up costing more than new production because it involves collection, transportation, and separation of the used materials. Another problem is that melting waste products requires very high temperatures, and waste gases are often a result. Solving the problem of one type of pollution can actually create pollution in another form!

Recycling trash is helpful, even though it is not perfect. Do not give up hope, however, because scientists and researchers are continuing to look for better solutions and techniques to improve the recycling process.

1. What is the main idea of this story?
   A. Recycling is one way of decreasing pollution, but it does have some problems of its own.
   B. People do not like to separate their trash.
   C. Recycling is not a good idea.

2. Why shouldn't trash be burned or buried?

_____

_____

3. What does the word "recycle" mean?
   A. separating into piles of like materials
   B. able to break down into natural elements
   C. reprocessed and used again

4. What was an early problem with recycling methods?

_____

_____

5. Name three products that can be made from recycled paper:

_____

_____

6. Name two problems with recycling:

_____

_____

THINK AHEAD: What types of trash does your community recycle? Plan a trip to visit a recycling plant.

Pollution Controls

People are interested in protecting the environment from the effects of pollution. We all know that any damage to the environment will eventually be harmful to human life as well. Since it is humans who create most of the pollution, it is humans who must find a way to deal with it.

There are four ways to manage pollution that are currently being used. The first method is to stop pollution producers during periods of high air pollution. When the level of air pollution is higher than normal, some factories are forced to close until conditions improve. Some cities outlaw burning of any materials, even logs in a fireplace, when air pollution is heavy. By stopping major producers of pollution when levels are high, we give the environment a chance to lessen the problem on its own.

The second method of pollution control is to lessen the concentration of emissions, or waste given off. Some cities require workers to car pool to their jobs, reducing the number of vehicles giving off exhaust. Factories are required to build tall smokestacks so that the gases are released further away from the ground. This gives the wind a chance to spread the gases around, creating lower concentration in any one area. This method helps control smog in manufacturing areas, but by spreading the gas further it exposes even more people to the pollution. Taller smokestacks are also cited as a reason for the increase in acid rain.

Thirdly, some pollutants can be removed from waste products before they are released into the air or water. This method is called emissions reductions (reducing the amount of waste released). This method cuts back on the pollutants that can be released into the environment, but it also creates a new problem. When the pollutant has been removed from the waste it must be stored somewhere. It is usually put in air-tight containers then buried or stored in waste dumps. Scientists do not know what to do with this waste product, so it continues to build up. Recent laws concerning these waste products have prompted research for ways to treat the waste and make it harmless.

The fourth method of pollution control is to change the manufacturing process so that it produces less pollution from the start. Many new industries are finding ways to build factories that are more "environmentally friendly", creating much less waste products. This method of pollution control has proven to be more effective and less costly than the other three methods.

Controlling pollution is a complex and difficult problem. The very products that make life easier are creating dangerous conditions for the environment. Scientists and researchers know we cannot stop driving cars or manufacturing products. That is not a realistic solution. They are working on ways that will bring a balance back between the needs of man and the needs of the environment. If we keep trying new ideas and looking for better methods the problem of pollution may someday be no problem at all!

1. **What is the main idea of this story?**
   A. Taller smokestacks spread pollution even farther.
   B. Some dangerous waste products are stored in barrels and buried.
   C. People are working to control the levels of pollution.

2. **Why are people interested in protecting the environment from pollution?**

   _____

   _____

3. **In your own words, restate the four methods of pollution control:**

   _____

   _____

   _____

   _____

4. **Why is it useful for a factory to build a tall smoke stack?**

   _____

   _____

5. **What is a disadvantage of taller smoke stacks?**

   _____

6. **What is a problem with emissions reduction?**

   _____

   _____

7. **Car pools are an example of which method of pollution control?**

   _____

   _____

8. **What does the word "emission" mean?**
   A. changing the manufacturing process
   B. to give off
   C. reducing waste products

9. **Which pollution control method is believed to be most efficient?**

   _____

   _____

THINK AHEAD: Does your community have any "environmentally friendly" factories?

Endangered Animals

The dinosaurs that once roamed the earth have all disappeared. Everyone is aware that they are extinct now, but we are fascinated with what they must have been like. We cannot observe them to find out about their habits, nor can we know for certain what they looked like. All that we know about dinosaurs comes from guesses and theories we develop as their remains are found.

Dinosaurs are not the only animals that have become extinct. Once, North America was full of animals called mammoths. They looked a lot like the modern day elephant, but they were covered with long hair. Hunters found mammoths to be a rich source of food, skins for clothing, and bones for tools. There were so many mammoths that people did not worry about wasting the meat or skin. The mammoths could not reproduce quickly enough to replace the numbers that were killed by hunters. It did not take long to wipe out the entire species. Today we have a pretty good idea of what the mammoth looked like because ancient cave artists left us a few drawings of these beasts.

During the past few hundred years man has hunted many animals to extinction. The moas (large flightless birds) of New Zealand were easy to kill and tasted pretty good. It took only 200 years to make the moas extinct. Dodo birds were found in abundance on the Maritius Islands in the Indian Ocean. It was a strange looking bird with a large head and short legs. They could not move quickly and were unable to fly. Dodo birds were so easy to catch that it only took 70 years for them to become extinct. The Stellar's sea cow, related to the manatee, took only 27 years to become extinct!

Food was not the only reason animals have been hunted into extinction or near extinction. The Carolina parakeet had beautiful feathers that were popular fashion trends for hats. That bird became extinct because people thought it was pretty. Beavers were hunted for many years because their fur was used to make coats and hats. By 1800 the beaver population had dropped drastically and they were much more difficult to find. Fortunately trends changed about then, and beaver was no longer desirable. The beavers were saved, not because they were nearing extinction but, rather, because their fur was not in fashion!

Many other animals have become endangered, or close to extinction. In the 1920's, thousands of elephants were killed for their ivory tusks. The ivory was fashioned into piano keys and billiard balls. The bald eagle was considered quite a trophy to stuff and hang on walls. It was hunted until there were very few left. Whales, sea turtles, and panda bears are a few examples of animals on the endangered species list.

Animals, like all our other natural resources, are not limitless. When one species becomes extinct, it is not just that animal that is affected. Other animals that depended on that species for their own survival are affected, too. The entire ecological system is changed because of the disappearance of one species. The Endangered Species Act of 1973 is a law created to protect animals in danger of becoming extinct. The Act makes it a crime for anyone to sell or transport endangered animals or products made from endangered animals. The law also sets aside certain lands that are natural habitats (living areas) of these animals. By protecting these animals, we can prevent the needless extinction of any more of our wildlife. Our descendants in the future will not need to rely on books and pictures to tell them what elephants and whales looked like. They will be able to see the animals for themselves.

1. **What is the main idea of this story?**
   A. Dodo birds are extinct.
   B. It is important to prevent animals from becoming extinct.
   C. The Endangered Species Act protects endangered animals.

2. **What was the cause for the extinction of many animals?**

   _____

   _____

3. **Name four animals that are now extinct:**

   _____

   _____

4. **What does the word "habitat" mean?**
   A. place where a plant or animal naturally lives
   B. near extinction
   C. a law protecting animals

5. **Name three animals that are on the endangered species list:**

   _____

   _____

6. **Why is it important to save animals from extinction?**

   _____

   _____

THINK AHEAD: What areas near your community are protected as a habitat for endangered species?

National Parks

National parks are huge areas of land set aside to preserve the natural flora (plants) and fauna (animals). These parks are protected by law so that no one can use them for profit. People who go to national parks are considered to be visitors, and they are not allowed to hurt the animals or plants in any way. These parks are beautiful examples of nature at its best and are of great scientific, educational, and recreational value.

In the 1800's less than ten national parks existed in Canada, the United States, and Australia. As the world became aware of the dangers of pollution and extinction, many more parks were created to ensure that some of nature would remain in its original state. Since 1990, more than 100 countries have established national parks or reserves and there are now more than 2,000 such parks around the world!

Canada's first national park was established in 1885. Banff National Park in Alberta sits in the Rocky Mountains near the British Colombian border. It is known for its beautiful mountains, its glaciers, Lake Louise, and variety of wildlife. The United States established its first national park, Yellowstone, in 1872. It covers a large area that includes parts of Idaho, Montana, and Wyoming. Yellowstone is best known for having numerous geysers and hot springs, and for its breathtaking scenery. Australia established its first park in 1879.

The idea of national parks caught on and many were established during the late 1800's and early 1900's. New Zealand, South Africa, Sweden, Russia, France, and Switzerland were among the first countries to recognize the value of such reserves and quickly established their own. The world's highest mountains, largest waterfalls, and other important natural features on nearly every continent are now protected as national parks. Governments are eager to set aside as many parks as possible before civilization takes over and changes them forever.

National parks have run into several problems in protecting their natural environment, however. When native animals are given complete protection, as they are in national parks, they can reproduce rapidly and soon become a problem. For example, the Yellowstone elk and the African elephant have become so large in number they are endangering the survival of some plants and other smaller animals in the park! Another problem is the large number of visitors to the parks each year. So many tourists are attracted to the parks that control over misuse is difficult to enforce. The huge size of some parks makes them easy targets for poachers (illegal hunters).

Even with the problems that face them, national parks are wonderful areas that can make people appreciate nature and learn more about the world we live in. They are there for us to visit and enjoy. They will be there for future generations to visit and learn from as well!

1. **What is the main idea of this story?**
   A. National parks can be found all over the world.
   B. National parks are places set aside to preserve nature.
   C. Many plants and animals are safe in national parks.

2. **What are national parks?**

   _____

   _____

3. **How many national parks existed in the 1880's?**

   _____

   _____

4. **What is Banff National Park known for?**

   _____

   _____

5. **What does the word "fauna" mean?**
   A. plants
   B. wildlife
   C. national parks

6. **Name two problems that national parks must deal with:**

   _____

   _____

7. **Where would you find Banff National Park?**

   _____

   _____

8. **What is Yellowstone National Park famous for?**

   _____

   _____

9. **What is a poacher?**
   A. a fried egg
   B. an angry deer
   C. an illegal hunter

THINK AHEAD: What national park is closest to where you live? What are its outstanding features?

Transportation

From ancient times to today, people have tried to find better ways to transport themselves and their things from one place to another. The first major improvement of land transportation was when man began to domesticate, or tame, animals. Horses and mules were perfect for carrying a tired person or a load of items too heavy for one person to handle. The invention of the wheel was probably the second and most important step in transportation. The wheel allowed people to roll wagons and carts easily. When animals were attached to the cart, whole loads of heavy items could be moved at one time. Of course, the paths made for walking of animals was not wide enough for carts, so wider paths called roads were made. These wonderful inventions allowed people to travel at the quick pace of about six miles per hour. Carts, animals, and roads sure beat walking! Land transportation did not change much over the next three or four thousand years. There were some improvements like the horse collar and carriage springs, but the combination of animals and carts could not be outdone until the invention of trains during the 17th century. The first trains were horse-drawn wagons with wooden wheels and rails, used mainly in mining.

Water transportation probably began around the same time as domestic animal transportation. Someone probably noticed that a log would float in the water and climbed on the first boat! Little is known about early boats, but at some time the log was hollowed out and shaped to make it more stable. Eventually pushing sticks or paddles were added to make the boat move more rapidly through the water. Larger ships controlled by many oars and propelled, or moved by sails, increased the ability to move about from one land to another. The invention of the rudder (a flat piece of wood or metal used to steer boats) and the compass gave water transportation a real boost. Now, even larger ships could be built and they dared to venture farther into the oceans in search of adventure.

The invention of the steam engine around 1698 was one of the largest improvements to transportation. By the late 1700's the steam engine propelled boats and trains, vastly improving the speed at which anyone could travel! Steam engines controlled transportation for about eighty years until the internal combustion engine (gasoline motor) was invented in 1860. By 1890, the first "horseless carriages" were introduced and in 1912 came the first motorized airplane. Transportation would never again be the same! The first rocket was launched in 1926, and by 1969 man had landed on the moon.

Today's road systems, railways, airplanes, and connected waterways provide the fast and fairly inexpensive transportation man has always looked for. The same cross-country trip that took a horse and wagon four months to complete can now be made by car in four days or by plane in four hours.

1. **What is the main idea of this story?**
   A. Faster and better transportation has always been important to people.
   B. Transportation did not really improve until the invention of the steam engine.
   C. Rockets are the fastest means of transportation ever invented.

2. **What was the first major improvement in land transportation?**

   _____

   _____

3. **What did the wheel allow people to do?**

   _____

   _____

4. **How long did animals and carts remain as the best means of land transportation?**

   _____

   _____

5. **What did the first trains consist of?**

   _____

   _____

6. **What does the word "propel" mean?**
   A. to tame
   B. to move forward
   C. to steer or guide

7. **Which two inventions allowed sailors to travel the oceans?**

   _____

   _____

8. **What does the word "rudder" mean?**
   A. to move forward
   B. to steer or guide
   C. a flat piece of wood or metal used to steer boats and ships

9. **How did the invention of the steam engine change transportation?**

   _____

   _____

THINK AHEAD: What types of transportation have you used? What do you predict transportation will be like 100 years from now?

Roads and Highways

Getting from one point to another is much easier if there is a path or road. Think about walking through the woods. Trying to get around trees and through bushes is a difficult task. It is much easier to get where you are going if a path or trail has been cleared for you. Early travelers had much the same problem. The first person to walk through an area had to clear the way, or create a route. When people began to use carts and wagons, these paths had to be widened so the wheels could fit. Motorized vehicles were wider still than carts and wagons, thus making the roads even wider.

There are many words that describe different types of land routes. Tracks were probably the first type of route. A track is a route that is not terribly well marked, but is evident. If you have ever followed an animal by watching for the footprints, you have been on a track. A track that is used often and is clearly evident is called a path. A trail is a path that has been well worn until the ground has been packed down. A road is a narrow route, usually wide enough for two cars, and is found in rural (country) areas. A street is much like a road, but is found in urban (city) areas. A highway has several lanes going in each direction and is divided by raised curbs or grassy areas. Highways that have limited access (not many ways to get on or off) are called expressways or freeways. If you must pay a toll, or fee, to drive on the expressway it is called a turnpike. Names used in other countries include motorway (Great Britain), autobahn (Germany), autostrada (Italy) and autoroute(France).

Dirt roads worked well with carts and wagons for a very long time, but they were often dusty and muddy. As motorized vehicles became popular, the need for better roads arose. Some cities solved the problem by paving the streets with bricks or small stones. This was a difficult and rather expensive job. Long stretches of road through rural areas were treated differently. The first attempts at paving were made by laying small trees or saplings next to each other across the road. As you can imagine, these roads were very bumpy and quickly became known as "corduroy roads". Corduroy roads were not very popular and were soon replaced with sawed boards called planks. These plank roads made vehicle travel much easier. They were smooth and removed the problems of dust, puddles, and ruts associated with dirt roads. In rural areas today there are paved roads that still go by the name "plank". In the early 19th century, France was the first country to begin paving their roads with asphalt. These roads were very popular because they were very smooth and were dust proof . It was soon discovered that when asphalt becomes wet it also becomes slippery. About 1929 the asphalt roads were given a top layer of rough material that prevented the road from becoming so slippery. Most roads and highways today are constructed of concrete poured over a wire mesh to make them stronger.

Today much of the world is crisscrossed with roads and highways that can take vehicles from the deserts of Egypt to the rainforests of Brazil. Travel is much easier than it was only 100 years ago. Just think what the next 100 years will bring!

1. **What is the main idea of this story?**
   A. Roads were first paved in 1929.
   B. Dirt roads were too dusty and bumpy for motorized vehicles.
   C. Roads have developed from dirt paths to multilane expressways.

2. **What is the difference between a road and a highway?**

   _____

   _____

3. **What is the difference between a corduroy and a plank road?**

   _____

   _____

4. **What does the word "urban" mean?**
   A. of the city
   B. of the country
   C. street

5. **Where would you find an "autoroute"?**
   A. France
   B. Canada
   C. in a forest

6. **Which country is credited with being the first to use asphalt as a road cover?**

   _____

   _____

7. **What was the main problem with asphalt roads?**

   _____

   _____

8. **Why do motorized vehicles need smoother roads than wagons and carts do?**

   _____

   _____

THINK AHEAD: Describe what you think the roads will be like 100 years from now.

World Highways

Roads allow us to go from place to place quickly and easily. Roads are connections from one place to another. They are used as an easy means to transport goods, carry messages, and visit other places. The importance of roads as connections between places was established many thousands of years ago.

As early as 3,000 B.C., road systems had been developed in Egypt and Mesopotamia. By 200 B.C., the Ch'in dynasty in China had built a road system that covered most of the country. The Incas of South America never discovered the wheel, and yet they had a well maintained road system that stretched about 2,300 miles! Early Romans recognized the importance of roads and established an excellent system that provided a connection for the entire empire.

Road systems continue to be an important link between towns, cities, and countries today. They provide easy access between places and have contributed greatly to international trade. Goods can be shipped quickly and inexpensively by highway. Today's highway systems are extensive and usually well maintained.

One of the longest highway systems in the world is the Pan American Highway. Construction on this highway began in 1923, and parts of it are still not completed. The Pan American Highway is about 26,000 miles long and connects Canada, the United States, Mexico, Central America, and South America. The highway crosses desert, dense tropical jungle, and high mountain passes. It has been mostly completed except for two sections - the isthmus of Panama and the Darien Gap. The Pan American Highway ends in Santiago in central Chile.

Many countries have excellent highway systems. Germany has constructed a highway system that extends about 2,500 miles between Bonn and Cologne. The Autobahn was begun under Hitler, but grew considerably after World War II. The motorway was built with fast travel in mind so there are no speed limits. Canada has several important national and international roadways. The Trans-Canada Highway was begun in 1962 and completed in 1965. Covering 4,860 miles, it is the longest national highway in the world. Another Canadian highway, the Alaska Highway, was built to connect Alaska with the continental United States. This roadway extends 2,452 miles from Dawson Creek, British Columbia to Fairbanks, Alaska. It was first used a military supply route, but was opened to the public in 1947.

Although speed is an important factor of highways, it is not the only consideration. Driving along stretches of road can become very boring and cause the driver to become sleepy. Modern highway planners try to select areas that are suitable to construction and provide scenic areas that help to keep drivers alert. Another problem for planners is how to connect road systems without destroying part of the city itself. Raised roadways, tunnels, and overpasses are designed so new roads can go over or under the land with little disruption to what is already there.

48   CD-3715

1. **What is the main idea of this story?**
   A. Road systems have been an important connection for people.
   B. The Trans-Canada Highway is the longest road in the world.
   C. Roads are designed for both speed and safety.

2. **Where were the earliest road systems built?**

_____

_____

3. **What is the importance of road systems?**

_____

_____

4. **What is the longest national highway in the world?**

_____

5. **Which highway system links all of the American countries?**

_____

6. **Name three large highway systems:**

_____

_____

7. **What two area does the Alaska Highway connect? What was it first used for?**

_____

_____

8. **How do highway planners avoid tearing down everything in order to build new roads?**

_____

_____

_____

9. **What kinds of areas do highway planners try to select for building new highways? Why?**

_____

_____

_____

THINK AHEAD: What international highway system is closest to where you live?

Name _____

Bridges

A problem that faced all road builders was how to span natural obstacles, or things that were in the way. Roads were built across all kinds of terrain from mountains to ravines to rivers. One structure that helped cross ravines and rivers was the bridge. The earliest bridges were probably tree trunks or flat stones thrown across a stream. This method of providing a span is known as beam bridges. As better means of transportation developed, so did the need for better bridges.

Early bridges were also built by suspension, or hanging. These bridges consisted of twisted bamboo or vines tied to tree trunks on either side of the obstacle to be crossed. Thick sticks or boards were tied to the vines so they could be crossed easily. Bridges of this type can still be found in parts of Africa and Asia.

Some of the finest bridges of early times were constructed by the Romans. They gave us many of the building techniques that are still in use today. The Romans discovered a type of cement that could be used to build foundations that extended into the water. Roman bridges were semicircular arches that were made of stone or brick. This method of construction is known as arch bridges. The Roman bridges were impressive, some standing as tall as 98 feet high. These bridges were very well built and many are still standing today.

The 14th through the 16th centuries was another great era for building bridges. Advancements were made in methods of anchoring, or holding the bridge in place, across fairly long distances. Arches were designed to be large enough so that ships might pass under them. Piles were driven into the water to provide a support for the arch ends where they came down into the water. Bridges became like works of art to be enjoyed as well as useful. Several wide bridges built during this time were wide enough to allow room for small shops along the sides!

The use of iron during the 18th and 19th centuries made bridge designing easier than ever. Iron could be shaped, bolted together, and was very strong. In 1791 the first all iron bridge was built over the River Severn in England. The use of iron also allowed suspension bridges to hold a great deal of weight. Strong metal cables were used to support two lanes of roadway over distances of up to 600 feet. The finest example of the early suspension bridge is the Brooklyn Bridge built in the late 1800's. Four main cables support six lanes of traffic and a wide footbridge that spans almost 1,600 feet! The Brooklyn Bridge is still an important connection between Brooklyn and Manhattan.

Many modern bridges must be movable to allow large ships to pass. Vehicles are stopped while sections of the bridge are moved for water traffic. Bascule bridges swing upward at one end or in the middle to create an opening. Lift bridges have a section that remains horizontal while weights at each end are lowered, lifting the bridge section high above the water. Other bridges rest on a pivot or pin. A section of the bridge actually turns sideways, allowing ships to pass beside it. The development of stronger supports allows new bridges to be built at such heights that even the tallest ships can easily pass under without interrupting the traffic.

1. **What is the main idea of this story?**
   A. Bridges have movable sections to allow ships to pass.
   B. Early bridges were made of stones or tree trunks.
   C. Bridges were built, allowing roads to be built over natural obstacles.

2. **What early people built the finest bridges for their time?**

   _____

   _____

3. **Another word for "suspension" is:**
   A. moving
   B. driving
   C. hanging

3. **How did the discovery of iron help build better bridges?**

   _____

   _____

4. **What does the word "obstacle" mean?**
   A. a bridge that swings sideways
   B. something that is in the way
   C. having strong anchors

5. **What three things were special about bridges built in the 14th, 15th, and 16th centuries?**

   _____

   _____

6. **Why was there a need for movable bridges?**

   _____

   _____

7. **What is a Bascule bridge?**

   _____

   _____

THINK AHEAD: Find the name of the longest single suspension bridge in the world.

London Bridge

Almost every small child has heard the nursery rhyme about London Bridge and how it is falling down. The rhyme was based on the actual history of this old bridge. London Bridge is the name of three bridges constructed in the same spot over the Thames River in England.

The first structure, called Old London Bridge, was built during the 1100's. It was among the last of the timber (wooden) bridges to be built over the Thames. Old London Bridge has 19 arches that rested on wide piers built in the river. The bridge was very wide and many wooden shops and homes were built along the sides. The bridge was damaged many times when the wooden buildings caught fire. This occurred so many times it seemed as though the bridge was constantly being rebuilt. The bridge "fell down" so many times it became the subject of the nursery rhyme. The shops and houses were finally removed from the bridge in 1763.

Old London Bridge was replaced by a five arched masonry (stone or brick) structure in 1831. The masonry bridge was replaced in 1967 with a six lane concrete bridge. The stone bridge was sold, carefully taken apart, and reconstructed in Lake Havasu City, Arizona where it stands today.

1. **What is the main idea of this story?**
    A. London Bridge was the name of three different bridges built in the same spot.
    B. London Bridge is the subject of a nursery rhyme.
    C. London Bridge burned many times.

2. **What was the biggest problem with Old London Bridge?**

_____

_____

3. **What happened to the second London Bridge?**

_____

_____

4. **When was the third London Bridge constructed?**

_____

5. **How many arches did Old London Bridge have? How many did the second London Bridge have?**

_____

_____

THINK AHEAD: What problems do you think might be caused by putting shops and homes on bridges today?

Tunnels

Road builders had a special challenge when they came to mountain areas. The roads had to climb gradually, turning and twisting as they went up or down the steep sides. Miles of road had to be laid just to cross over a few miles. During the 1800's the increasing use of railroads caused builders to consider new ideas about crossing the mountains. The most direct route was, of course, a tunnel straight through the mountain.

Digging a tunnel was not a new idea. Early cave dwellers tunneled to make a natural cave bigger. Babylonians dug tunnels for irrigation of crops. Egyptians created tunnels for tombs and temple rooms in the pyramids. The ancient Greeks used tunnels to bring water to their villages. One tunnel, built on the island of Samos in the 6th century B.C., was about 3,000 feet long. The Romans also dug a tunnel to connect the city of Pozzuoli with Naples. This tunnel, cut through rock, was 4,800 feet long and 25 feet wide.

During the 1800's tunneling techniques improved with the use of drills and dynamite. These methods were used to dig the 8.5 mile long Mont Cenis Tunnel through the mountains between Italy and France in 1857-71. At about the same time other major tunnels were being built elsewhere. The Hoosac Tunnel (1872-82) was built through the Berkshires in the United States. The First Simplon Tunnel (1898-1906) connected Italy and Switzerland with twelve miles of tunnel. The First Simplon held the record of the longest transportation tunnel in the world for many years.

As rock tunneling developed, so did the idea of subaqueous (under water) tunneling. Subaqueous tunnels are holes dug through the ground below a river or other body of water. A French engineer named Marc Brunel developed a shield for tunneling under rivers. The shield was a large rectangular box where 36 diggers could work at the same time. The first underwater tunnel was built in 1825-43 under the Thames River in England. In 1906-10 a new kind of tunnel connecting Detroit, Michigan and Windsor, Ontario was built in the Detroit River. This tunnel went through the water rather than under it. The tunnel was built in sections and sealed closed. The sections were sunk to the bottom of the river and connected together by divers. The tunnel was then covered for protection. Japanese railroad tunnels were the first tunnels built under the ocean (1936-44). The Seikan Tunnel connects the Japanese islands of Honshu and Hokkaido and is 33 miles long.

Subways are common tunnels found in most major cities. These tunnels are formed by digging deep trenches in the ground, building the tunnels, then covering the tunnel over with dirt. Subways provide an efficient method of transportation without using valuable ground space, as roads do.

1. **What is the main idea of this story?**
   A. The use of railroads created the need for tunnels.
   B. Tunnels were invented by cave dwellers.
   C. Tunnels provide direct transportation routes without using valuable above
      ground space.
2. **How must roads be constucted in mountain areas?**

   _____

   _____

3. **For what purpose did ancient Greeks build tunnels?**

   _____

4. **What did the 4,800 foot long Roman tunnel connect?**

   _____

   _____

5. **What two techniques improved tunneling during the 1800's?**

   _____

   _____

6. **What does the word "subaqueous" mean?**
   A. a tunnel for subways
   B. under water
   C. a Roman tunnel that carried water to villages
7. **Who invented the shield for tunneling under water?**

   _____

   _____

8. **How is the Detroit/Windsor tunnel different from most under water tunnels?**

   _____

   _____

7. **What were the first tunnels built under the ocean?**

   _____

   _____

THINK AHEAD: What is the longest subaqueous tunnel in the world today?

The Chunnel

The English Channel is a section of the Atlantic Ocean that separates England and France. It is 21 to 150 miles wide and 565 feet deep. The strong waves in the channel have often made passage across it dangerous. In the 1880's, advances in tunneling convinced the British to try to dig a tunnel under the channel. Efforts were abandoned at that time because the British were afraid that such a tunnel could be used in an invasion attempt. The idea came up again around 1970, but was once more put aside, this time in favor of developing the supersonic Concorde jet.

Until recently the main transportation across the English Channel has been ferry boats and hovercraft . In 1986, France and Great Britain decided to join in the construction of the tunnel under the channel. The popular name for this project has become the "Chunnel". The plan was to dig a railway tunnel with each country starting on their own side of the channel. Work began in 1988. On December 1, 1990 the digging crews on both sides finally met in the middle of the channel. The Chunnel was opened for use in 1994.

1. **What is the main idea of this story?**
     A. The Chunnel is a railway tunnel.
     B. The French and English dug a tunnel.
     C. The Chunnel is a railway tunnel connecting France and England.

2. **How wide is the English Channel?**

_____

3. **When did the British first decide to dig a tunnel under the channel?**

_____

_____

4. **What was the main means of transportation across the channel before the Chunnel was opened?**

_____

_____

5. **When did the Chunnel open for public use?**

_____

THINK AHEAD: Find out more about the Chunnel. How long is it? How long does it take to cross the channel using the chunnel?

Canals

Canals are man-made channels constructed for three main purposes. First, some canals are built for drainage of excess water. For example, the city of New Orleans in Louisiana has a canal drainage system. After a heavy rain the excess water is directed to the canals through drainpipes. The canals move the water toward pumping stations located on the Mississippi River and Lake Pontchartrain. The pumping stations pump the excess water over the levees (protective walls) and dump it into the river and lake. The canal systems help keep the city from flooding.

A second use for canals is to help ships bypass hazards on rivers. Canals of this type are most often used when the water level suddenly changes, usually near falls or rapids. Devices called locks are used in situations like these. Locks are like elevators for ships. A series of heavy doors are used to create a temporary dam across the water. To illustrate the point, imagine a ship on the higher side of a small waterfall. It certainly cannot go over the falls to continue its journey, so it is guided into a canal that goes around the falls. In the middle of the canal stands a heavy metal door, the first door on the lock. The door opens, the ship enters, and the door closes behind it. At the other end of the lock is another heavy metal door which is closed. The water level in the lock is the same as the high side of the falls. As the ship sits in the lock, water is slowly released and the water level begins to drop. When the water level is equal to the level below the falls the second door opens and the ship leaves. When a ship needs to go from the lower level to the higher level, water is pumped into the lock until it matches the higher water level.

For thousands of years water has been an important and inexpensive means for transporting large cargoes or cargoes that do not require fast delivery. Cargo such as coal, timber, grain, and chemicals can be loaded onto ships in large quantities and transported across oceans to the countries where they are needed. Getting the cargo inland where it would be used presented some problems, however. Some large ports were on inland waterways and there was no reasonable way to reach them. Canals have helped to solve this problem.

A third use for canals is to link bodies of water together. These are called ship or sea canals and can be found in many places around the world. Famous examples are the Suez Canal joining Africa and Asia, the Panama Canal joining the Atlantic and Pacific Oceans, the Erie Canal connecting Lake Erie and the Hudson River, and the Welland Canal linking Lake Ontario and Lake Erie. These canals provide an important link between manufacturing areas and the seaports where raw materials are imported.

1. **What is the main idea of this story?**
   A. Canals link bodies of water to one another.
   B. Canals are used in three important ways.
   C. Canals are used to transport goods by water.

2. **Name the three uses for canals described in this passage:**

   _____

   _____

   _____

3. **What are locks used for?**

   _____

   _____

4. **What does the word "levee" mean?**
   A. drainage canal
   B. to transport by canal
   C. a protective wall to keep water out

5. **What is the reason for connecting large bodies of water?**

   _____

   _____

6. **Name three major canals:**

   _____

   _____

   _____

THINK AHEAD: Which canal is the longest in the world? Where is it located?

Suez and Panama Canals

Two of the most important canals in the world are the Suez and the Panama. The Suez Canal is located between Asia and Africa, helping to link the Mediterranean Sea, the Red Sea, and the Indian Ocean. Before this canal was opened in 1869, European and East African ships that wanted to go to the Far East had to sail all the way around Africa. The Suez Canal provided a shorter route, cutting the distance in half in some cases. By 1888 the canal was recognized as an important world route and all ships of all nations were guaranteed freedom to use it.

The Suez Canal is owned and operated by Egypt. It begins at Port Said and ends at Port Taufiq, cutting across marshes and desert areas. The canal is 105 miles long and takes about 15 hours to go from one end to the other. During the 1960's about 15 percent of all world trade came through the Suez Canal. A great deal of that trade was petroleum (raw oil) that came from the Persian Gulf. As the world became more dependent on oil, ships called supertankers were created to transport larger quantities. The Suez Canal was too narrow for these big ships, and use of the canal dropped. Between 1975 and 1980 only about 4 percent of the world trade passed through the Suez Canal. Since that time the canal has been widened and deepened to accommodate these larger ships.

The Panama Canal crosses the Isthmus of Panama to connect the Atlantic and Pacific Oceans. Early sailors had to go around South America to get from one ocean to the other. The idea of building a canal across Panama originated during the early 16th century, but the technology to do it had not yet been developed. In 1881 a French company bought the rights to the canal and began to dig. The land was difficult to clear and many workers suffered from malaria or yellow fever. Work on the canal came to a halt in 1887. In 1904 the United States bought the rights to build the canal. By 1904 they had begun construction and completed the project in 1914. The total cost of the canal was about 3.5 million dollars.

Because of the difficult land and the great distance the canal covered, it was hailed as the greatest engineering creation of the modern age. The canal is 7,000 miles long, 300 feet wide, and at least 41 feet deep. Cristobal is the city that sits on the Atlantic side with Balboa on the Pacific. The canal has six sets of locks that raise and lower the ships to the proper level for each ocean. It takes about eight hours to cross from one ocean to the other.

The canal continued to be a great success for many years. During the 1970's and 80's, however, the development of wider ships created problems for passage through the canal. Work to widen the canal began in 1991, but is not yet completed.

1. **What is the main idea of this story?**
   A. The Suez and Panama Canals are important world water routes.
   B. The Panama Canal is longer than the Suez Canal.
   C. The Suez Canal was built before the Panama Canal.

2. **How did European and East African ships reach the Far East before the Suez Canal was built?**

   _____

3. **Why did use of the Suez Canal drop between 1975 and 1980?**

   _____

   _____

4. **In what year did each of the canals open?**

   _____

5. **What is the length of each canal?**

   _____

   _____

6. **What does the word "petroleum" mean?**
   A. a water route across desert land
   B. raw oil
   C. malaria

7. **Who began work on the Panama Canal in 1881?**

   _____

8. **Why did work on the Panama Canal stop in 1887?**

   _____

   _____

9. **What was the final cost of building the Panama Canal?**

   _____

10. **What bodies of water does each of the canals connect?**

   _____

   _____

THINK AHEAD: Look at a map of North and South America. Explain why early sailors felt Panama was a good place to dig a canal.

Railroads

Railroads were first introduced in the 1500's and were used in England's mining operations. These first "trains" were wagons set on wooden rails and pulled by horses. During the 1700's they became more useful when they were outfitted with cast-iron wheels and rails, but they still were not very popular modes of transportation. The invention of the steam engine during the mid 1700's was just what the trains needed to become successful. The first public transportation railway was opened in 1825 in England. This 20 mile railroad opened the world's eyes to a new mode of transportation, the steam powered train.

It did not take long for people to realize that travel by train was superior to wagons, canals, and even steamboats. Trains were faster and more direct than water routes, cheaper and easier than wagon travel, and dependable throughout the year. During the 1800's, railroads began to pop up all over the world. France, Belgium, Germany, Italy, the Netherlands, and Russia all had railroads in operation by 1830. Canada opened its first rail service in 1836, and by 1880 had almost 7,000 miles of track. The Canadian Pacific Railway was completed across the Rockies to the Pacific by 1885. In 1860 the United States had over 30,000 miles of rail crossing the country.

Early passenger cars were similar to stagecoaches or wagons. Before long the cars were lengthened and could hold 40 to 50 people. Around 1860, sleeping cars were introduced so passengers could stretch out and relax on their journey. In the late 1860's, George Pullman designed dining and sleeping cars for railway lines. They were elaborate and comfortable, setting the standard of passenger cars for many years. By 1890 many coaches (passenger cars) were equipped with electric lights, heat, and covered passageways between cars.

Longer and heavier cars created a need for stronger locomotives, or engines. By the early 1900's the steam engine was being replaced with electric locomotives for high speed trains and diesel-electric locomotives for long distance travel. In 1964 the Japanese began to operate the now famous electric engine "bullet" train. It is capable of traveling at speeds up to 160 miles per hour. The trains have 16 cars that are permanently linked together and have four motors each. In 1981 The French completed a train which travels over steep inclines going as fast as 170 miles per hour.

The most recent train design does not have steel tracks or wheels. As a matter of fact it has no wheels at all! The Maglev (magnetic levitation train) glides over a magnetic field that raises it above the track. Other magnetic systems guide the train, make it stop, or add speed when needed. The Germans and the Japanese have been working to perfect this new train. Experimental models of the Maglev have traveled at speeds up to 300 miles per hour!

1. **What is the main idea of this story?**
   A. Trains are cheaper and faster than wagons.
   B. Railroads have been an important means of transportation throughout the world.
   C. The steam engine helped the popularity of trains.
2. **Describe the very first railroad:**

   _____

   _____

3. **In what ways were trains better than other modes of transportation?**

   _____

   _____

4. **What does the word "coaches" mean in this passage?**
   A. teachers
   B. trains with wooden tracks
   C. passenger cars of a train
5. **How had trains been improved by 1890?**

   _____

   _____

6. **What change was made to locomotives in the early 1900's?**

   _____

7. **Why did electric locomotives become necessary?**

   _____

   _____

8. **How fast does the Japanese "bullet" travel?**

   _____

9. **What makes the Maglev travel so fast?**

   _____

   _____

THINK AHEAD: How do you think the Maglev will affect the way people travel in the future?

Above and Below Ground

In 1850, the common mode of local transportation was the horse and carriage. Major cities experienced the first traffic jams as the streets filled with carriages each day. It was apparent that cities needed to find an efficient way to move large quantities of people in shorter time periods. This was the birth of rapid transit systems (quick transport). Trains had become the most common means of transportation at this time, so it was only natural that cities looked to them as a solution.

In 1863, London became the first city to boast an underground railway system which quickly became known as the "tube". The subway had been born! Streets were removed while tunnels were dug below them. The walls and ceiling of the tunnel were constructed then covered with dirt. The roads were replaced directly over the tunnel. This is the most common way to build a subway and has been aptly named the "cut and cover" method. The subway worked well and soon other cities were building them as well.

New York City was also deeply congested with traffic and the idea of a subway interested them. However, Manhattan was built on granite, a very hard rock, and digging tunnels was not a wise idea at the time. Instead, New York looked up for the answer to their traffic problems. By 1868 New York had constructed elevated railways, commonly known as "els", that ran above the streets rather than under them. Els were railroad tracks that ran on a platform held above the streets by steel or concrete columns. Other cities, like Chicago, that had difficulty with tunneling also constructed elevated railways. The subway was far more popular in Europe, but only Hamburg and Liverpool built elevated systems.

These first rapid transit subways and els were powered by a steam engine locomotive, just as the regular ground trains were. They pulled between two and ten wooden passenger cars, or coaches. Each coach had several doors so the train could be quickly loaded and unloaded. The steam released from the locomotive created some operating problems, especially inside the subway tunnels. By 1890 the old steam engines were replaced by the cleaner and more efficient electric motors. A third track conducting electricity was placed next to the train tracks, supplying the train with electricity to move. Electricity is still used to power most subways today. Operators control the speed of the train by regulating the amount of electricity the motors receive.

By 1945, tunneling techniques had improved and New York began to build subways as well. The elevated trains were replaced by the subway in Manhattan, but remained in many suburbs of the city and are still in use today. Many portions of Chicago's el were also removed, but the "loop" in the middle of the city is still very busy.

Today, every major capital in the world has a subway system. Many are unique in the way they have made their subway safe or pleasant. Mexico City suspended their tunnels to absorb shock waves from earthquakes. Montreal uses rubber tires on their subway, making it the quietest one in the world. Hong Kong has the first fully air conditioned subway. These underground trains move thousands of people each day and have indeed lived up to their title of "rapid transit".

1. What is the main idea of this story?
   A. In 1850 cities experience their first traffic jams.
   B. More cities prefer subways to elevated trains.
   C. Elevated trains and subways are two forms of rapid transit systems.

2. Why was rapid transit needed as early as 1850?

_____

_____

3. Which city had the first subway, and what year was it built?

_____

4. What does the word "granite" mean?
   A. a third track conducting electricity
   B. a type of rock
   C. a method of digging subway tunnels

5. What powered the first subways and elevated trains?

_____

_____

6. Describe the first coaches:

_____

_____

7. Which two European cities built an elevated system?

_____

8. What is unique about Montreal's subway?

_____

THINK AHEAD: How do you think the used of magnetically powered trains (like the Maglev) will affect subway transportation?

Cloze is a reading exercise where some of the words are missing and you must put them back in. Read the story below. Every tenth word has been taken out and is listed below the passage. Fill in the blanks with the words you think will make sense.

a	far	go	had	had	I	I	It	looked	many	mile
morning	Saturday	The	the	the	the	when	worn			

Lost!

The cold wind was bitter so I pulled my coat even tighter around my neck. Thank goodness I had followed my mother's advice and _____ mittens and a hat. Little did I know this _____ I would end up lost in the woods during _____ snowstorm! The day had started out so nicely. Cindy _____ invited me to her house for lunch and, being _____ with nothing to do, I immediately said I would _____. The sun was shining and the snow covered trees_____ so beautiful as I set out across the woods. _____ path was snowy, but packed down because Cindy and _____ had dragged our sleds over it so many times _____ past few days. Besides, it was only a half _____ to Cindy's house and I had walked the trail _____ times I would have known the way even without _____ trail. When I got to her house, Cindy and _____ had hot chocolate and played in the back yard. _____ was early after-noon when I started for home, but _____ sky was dark and threatening to snow. The wind _____ picked up, too. I was barely into the woods _____ the blizzard hit, making it difficult to see very _____ ahead. The trail was quickly lost under the falling snow. Now I was lost and had no idea which way to go.

Cloze is a reading exercise where some of the words are missing and you must put them back in. Read the story below. Every tenth word has been taken out and is listed below the passage. Fill in the blanks with the words you think will make sense.

a	a	best	each	front	her	if	made	nip	of
round	that	The	the	the	There	they	This

Fish

The fish swam soothingly through the water in the tank. I had been watching them for almost an hour. _____ was something peaceful and calming about the fish that _____ me feel good. I was even beginning to feel _____ I knew each individual fish as if it were _____ friend! The orange and white fish stayed together all _____ time. It was funny to watch the one in _____ turn quickly while the other three followed. I thought _____ might bump into each other, but they never did.

_____ two large yellow fish seemed to stay away from _____ other. If one came too near, the other would _____ at its tail or fin. They reminded me of _____ couple having a quarrel. The fish I liked the _____ was the smallest one of all. She had a _____ shape with a white front and a black tail. _____ little fish was hiding among the rocks most of _____ time. Every few minutes she would dart out, as _____ she might join the others. As soon as any _____ the other fish came near she would return to _____ hiding spot. I could almost imagine that I was a fish swimming in there with them!

65

Name _____

Skill: cloze

Cloze is a reading exercise where some of the words are missing and you must put them back in. Read the story below. Every tenth word has been taken out and is listed below the passage. Fill in the blanks with the words you think will make sense.

book	had	he	he	Last	meant	planned	promised	really
relatives		study	test		they	was	worried	

The Test

Marty wiped the sweat from his face and looked at the clock. Class would begin in one minute and Marty was _____ . Today Ms. Freble was giving the class a geography _____ and Marty was not at all prepared. He had _____ to study, but things kept getting in the way. _____ Thursday he took his book and notes home and _____ to look through them. Then Max came over and _____ played pool instead. Marty was not worried then because _____ still had three days left for studying. Friday night _____ the basketball game so, of course, he could not _____ then. Saturday Marty got as far as opening his _____ when Brian called. They went to the movie Marty _____ wanted to see and got home pretty late. Marty _____ himself he would study the next day. Was it _____ his fault that his parents decided to go visit _____ ? Marty knew he could not think about geography when _____ was busy talking to his cousin. Now here it was, Monday, and Marty had not even looked at his notes.

Name _____   Skill: *cloze*

Cloze is a reading exercise where some of the words are missing and you must put them back in. Read the story below. Every tenth word has been taken out and is listed below the passage. Fill in the blanks with the words you think will make sense.

an	and	animal	by	just	lumbered	perfect	quietly	silver	small
snuggled	sticks	The	the	their	through	two	up	watched	water

were   where

Univited Guest

R.J. and Michael dragged the heavy bag of supplies across the lawn and pushed it into the tent. That was the last of what they needed for _____ camp out in the backyard. The boys had erected _____ tent early in the morning. They set it out _____ the pond so they could barely see the house _____ the trees. The brothers had planned this event for _____ weeks so they were sure that everything would be _____ ! As the day turned into dusk, R.J. built a _____ fire and Michael took out the frankfurters and roasting _____ . Dinner was delicious. Soon it was dark and stars _____ shining from a million different spots in the sky. _____ moon was full and its bright light cast a _____ glow on the tent. Frogs began their night croaking _____ crickets hummed in the grass. Suddenly Michael sat straight _____ and quietly pointed at the pond. R.J. looked to _____ Michael was pointing and saw the shadowy shape of _____ animal at the edge of the water. They heard _____ splash as the animal took a drink. Then it _____ across the yard, straight for their tent. As the _____ came nearer, the glow from the dying fire cast _____ enough light to see what it was. The boys _____ as the huge skunk walked into their tent and _____ down on a sleeping bag. The boys got up _____ and headed for the house. They knew that they could not have planned anything to avoid this situation!

©1995 Kelley Wingate Publications   67   CD-3715

Cloze is a reading exercise where some of the words are missing and you must put them back in. Read the story below. Every eighth word has been taken out and is listed below the passage. Fill in the blanks with the words you think will make sense.

America	Arabian	called	countries	do	eating	fingers	is	meals	of
one	other	people	spoon	spoons	tables	their	times	use	

Eating Out

When you eat and how you eat depends on where you live. Meal times and utensils are a matter _____ custom, or what our culture has decided _____ best for the way we live. Many _____ eat three meals a day. They are _____ breakfast, lunch, and dinner (or supper). Some _____ countries, like England and Norway, eat four _____ a day. They have an afternoon "tea", _____ dinner much later in the evening. Most _____ use utensils to eat formal meals. North _____ and most of Europe sit down at _____ and eat with a knife, fork, and _____ . The eastern countries of Asia prefer to _____ chopsticks and bowls for their food. They _____ not use knives at the table because _____ food is prepared in small pieces. Many _____ families in the Middle East eat from _____ large bowl, using either their fingers or _____ . Most places in the world use their _____ to eat certain foods or at special _____ . Can you imagine trying to eat a hamburger with a knife and fork?

Cloze is a reading exercise where some of the words are missing and you must put them back in. Read the story below. Every eighth word has been taken out and is listed below the passage. Fill in the blanks with the words you think will make sense.

allowing	are	birds	can	from	in	inserted	living	narrow
nuts	of	on	or	parrot	sip	small	that	their

Bills are Tools

The bill of a bird can tell you a lot about what it eats and how it gets its food. The heron has a long pointed bill _____ looks like a spear. This bird wades _____ shallow water and spears passing fish. Some _____ , like the spoonbill, have long bills that _____ flattened near the tip. They can use _____ odd shaped bill to shovel small fish _____ mud or water. The shorter pointed bill _____ the woodpecker is used like a chisel _____ drill. They poke small holes into trees, _____ the woodpecker to expose the tiny insects _____ under the bark. The sparrow and robin have _____ bills that act as tweezers. These birds _____ easily pick up seeds and insects found _____ the ground. The hummingbird has a long _____ bill, like a straw. The bill is _____ deep into a flower and used to _____ nectar. A strong hooked bill, like the _____ has, is useful in cracking seeds and _____ with hard shells. Next time you are bird watching, see if you can figure out how the bird uses its bill.

Cloze is a reading exercise where some of the words are missing and you must put them back in. Read the story below. Every eighth word has been taken out and is listed below the passage. Fill in the blanks with the words you think will make sense.

also	As	because	caves	deep	developed	fish	fish
food	have	most	spent	themselves	there	they	

Cave Fish

One of the strangest types of fish is called the cave fish. These fish have been found deep in _____ all over the world. What makes this _____ so strange is that it is blind. _____ a matter of fact, some cave fish _____ no eyes at all! These fish have _____ their entire lives in pools or lakes _____ under the ground. There is no light _____ , so even if the fish had eyes _____ would be of little use. The cave _____ are far from helpless, however. They have _____ keen senses of smell and touch so _____ can be found easily. These strong senses _____ enable the fish to avoid being caught _____ . These animals have pale, almost invisible skin _____ they lack the skin pigment necessary in _____ animals as protection from the sun. These fish are living examples of how animals can adapt to their environment.

Cloze is a reading exercise where some of the words are missing and you must put them back in. Read the story below. Every eighth word has been taken out and is listed below the passage. Fill in the blanks with the words you think will make sense.

and	anything	arms	did	disappeared	done	feeling	He	he
inch	pile	skates	stepped	the	wanted	was	wet	

Hockey

A fresh snow had fallen during the night. Hal was busily shoveling the side of _____ pond where the ice had frozen solid. _____ lifted shovel after shovel of the heavy _____ snow and carried it over the the _____ he was making on the bank. Hal _____ not like to shovel snow, but there _____ no other way to get the job _____ . Before long the ice was cleared. Hal's _____ ached as he pulled off his boots _____ slipped his feet into a pair of _____ . He picked up his hockey stick and _____ onto the cleared ice. Pain and fatigue _____ as Hal glided across the smooth surface, _____ the cold wind against his cheeks. Every _____ of his body came to life as _____ guided the puck with his stick. Hal _____ to be a hockey player more than _____ else in the world. This was his dream, and Hal was willing to do whatever might take to make that dream come true.

Cloze is a reading exercise where some of the words are missing and you must put them back in. Read the story below. Every fifth word has been taken out and is listed below the passage. Fill in the blanks with the words you think will make sense.

a	a	all	at	because	family	have	hotel	I	In
My	national	near	other	part	picked	reads	so		
the	the	to	to	to	vacation	vote	what		

Family Vacation

It is a lot of fun to take a trip to new places. Planning the trip is

_____ of the excitement. My _____ looks at maps and

_____ books about different places. _____ June we each

pick _____ place we would like _____ go for our summer

_____ . Then we tell each _____ about the place we

_____ chosen. We talk about _____ things we can do

_____ the place we have _____ . Dad always chooses a

_____ park because he likes _____ camp. Mom usually

picks _____ city with a nice _____ and lots of museums.

_____ brother chooses a place _____ a lake or river

_____ he likes to fish. _____ change hobbies every year,

_____ you can never tell _____ area I will select! When

_____ family has heard about _____ the different places we

_____ on where we want _____ go. No matter what the

decision is, we all agree that our vacations are a lot of fun.

Cloze is a reading exercise where some of the words are missing and you must put them back in. Read the story below. Every fifth word has been taken out and is listed below the passage. Fill in the blanks with the words you think will make sense.

and	bent	compete	five	golf	hit	is	large	on	Players	playing
sand	Scottish	spread	to	use	wanted	what	where	with		

Golf

The Romans invented one sport called paganica that has developed into a popular sport today. The Roman emperors enjoyed _____ this game when they _____ to relax. They would _____ a bent stick to _____ a soft ball stuffed _____ feathers. For the next _____ hundred years the game _____ and was further developed _____ several different continents. The _____ refined the game into _____ we know today as _____ Today we use metal _____ wooden clubs instead of _____ sticks. The course (place _____ the game is played) _____ usually filled with trees, _____ pits, and water holes _____ make the game challenging. _____ from around the world _____ in this game for _____ cash prizes. Although the game is not quite the same as the Romans played it, it is still a relaxing and fun sport.

An affix is any letter or group of letters added to a word. If the affix is at the beginning of the word, it is a *prefix*. If it is added to the end of a word, it is a *suffix*. Below is a list of the most common affixes.

PREFIXES: ab- ad- be- com- de- dis- en- em- in- pre- pro- re- sub- un-
SUFFIXES: -ion -ition -ation -ful -less -ic -an -ian -n -al -ary -y -ance -ant -ence -er -ness -ment -able -ible -en -ous -ure -ity -ly -ive -s -es -d -ed -ing

These affixes may be added to a root word to form another word. Listed below are four words to which an affix has been added. Identify the root word and write it on the first line. Then make five more words by adding a different affix.

A. comparable

root word_____   1._____

2. _____   3. _____

4._____   5._____

B. disorderly

root word_____   1. _____

2._____   3. _____

4. _____   5._____

C. mistaken

root word_____   1. _____

2._____   3. _____

4._____   5._____

D. talkative

root word_____   1. _____

2._____   3. _____

4. _____   5._____

An affix is any letter or group of letters added to a word. If the affix is at the beginning of the word, it is a *prefix*. If it is added to the end of a word, it is a *suffix*. Below is a list of the most common affixes.

PREFIXES: ab- ad- be- com- de- dis- en- em- in- pre- pro- re- sub- un-
SUFFIXES: -ion -ition -ation -ful -less -ic -an -ian -n -al -ary -y -ance -ant -ence -er -ness -ment -able -ible -en -ous -ure -ity -ly -ive -s -es -d -ed -ing

These affixes may be added to a root word to form another word. Listed below are four words to which an affix has been added. Identify the root word and write it on the first line. Then make five more words by adding a different affix.

A. recoil

root word_____   1._____

2. _____   3. _____

4._____   5._____

B. unmoved

root word_____   1. _____

2._____   3. _____

4. _____   5._____

C. tingly

root word_____   1. _____

2._____   3. _____

4. _____   5._____

D. spinner

root word_____   1. _____

2._____   3. _____

4. _____   5._____

An affix is any letter or group of letters added to a word. If the affix is at the beginning of the word, it is a *prefix*. If it is added to the end of a word, it is a *suffix*. Below is a list of the most common affixes.

PREFIXES: ab- ad- be- com- de- dis- en- em- in- pre- pro- re- sub- un-
SUFFIXES: -ion -ition -ation -ful -less -ic -an -ian -n -al -ary -y -ance -ant -ence -er -ness -ment -able -ible -en -ous -ure -ity -ly -ive -s -es -d -ed -ing

These affixes may be added to a root word to form another word. Listed below are four words to which an affix has been added. Identify the root word and write it on the first line. Then make five more words by adding a different affix.

A. repose

    root word_____   1._____

    2. _____   3. _____

    4._____   5._____

B. passable

    root word_____   1. _____

    2._____   3. _____

    4. _____   5._____

C. learner

    root word_____   1. _____

    2._____   3. _____

    4. _____   5._____

D. dazedly

    root word_____   1. _____

    2._____   3. _____

    4. _____   5._____

An affix is any letter or group of letters added to a word. If the affix is at the beginning of the word, it is a *prefix*. If it is added to the end of a word, it is a *suffix*. Below is a list of the most common affixes.

PREFIXES: ab- ad- be- com- de- dis- en- em- in- pre- pro- re- sub- un-
SUFFIXES: -ion -ition -ation -ful -less -ic -an -ian -n -al -ary -y -ance -ant -ence -er -ness -ment -able -ible -en -ous -ure -ity -ly -ive -s -es -d -ed -ing

These affixes may be added to a root word to form another word. Listed below are four words to which an affix has been added. Identify the root word and write it on the first line. Then make five more words by adding a different affix.

A. amazingly

root word_____   1._____

2. _____   3. _____

4._____   5._____

B. clippings

root word_____   1. _____

2._____   3. _____

4. _____   5._____

C. electrified

root word_____   1. _____

2._____   3. _____

4. _____   5._____

D. mistreated

root word_____   1. _____

2._____   3. _____

4. _____   5._____

An affix is any letter or group of letters added to a word. If the affix is at the beginning of the word, it is a *prefix*. If it is added to the end of a word, it is a *suffix*. Below is a list of the most common affixes.

PREFIXES: ab- ad- be- com- de- dis- en- em- in- pre- pro- re- sub- un-
SUFFIXES: -ion -ition -ation -ful -less -ic -an -ian -n -al -ary -y -ance -ant -ence -er -ness -ment -able -ible -en -ous -ure -ity -ly -ive -s -es -d -ed -ing

These affixes may be added to a root word to form another word. Listed below are four words to which an affix has been added. Identify the root word and write it on the first line. Then make five more words by adding a different affix.

A. specifically

root word_____ 1._____

2. _____ 3. _____

4._____ 5._____

B. preserver

root word_____ 1. _____

2._____ 3. _____

4. _____ 5._____

C. workings

root word_____ 1. _____

2._____ 3. _____

4. _____ 5._____

D. uninteresting

root word_____ 1. _____

2._____ 3. _____

4. _____ 5._____

An affix is any letter or group of letters added to a word. If the affix is at the beginning of the word, it is a _prefix_. If it is added to the end of a word, it is a _suffix_. Below is a list of the most common affixes.

PREFIXES: ab- ad- be- com- de- dis- en- em- in- pre- pro- re- sub- un-
SUFFIXES: -ion -ition -ation -ful -less -ic -an -ian -n -al -ary -y -ance -ant -ence -er -ness -ment -able -ible -en -ous -ure -ity -ly -ive -s -es -d -ed -ing

These affixes may be added to a root word to form another word. Listed below are four words to which an affix has been added. Identify the root word and write it on the first line. Then make five more words by adding a different affix.

A. thoughtless

root word_____   1._____

2. _____   3. _____

4._____   5._____

B. productive

root word_____   1. _____

2._____   3. _____

4. _____   5._____

C. insanity

root word_____   1. _____

2._____   3. _____

4. _____   5._____

D. flatness

root word_____   1. _____

2._____   3. _____

4. _____   5._____

An affix is any letter or group of letters added to a word. If the affix is at the beginning of the word, it is a *prefix*. If it is added to the end of a word, it is a *suffix*. Below is a list of the most common affixes.

PREFIXES: ab- ad- be- com- de- dis- en- em- in- pre- pro- re- sub- un-
SUFFIXES: -ion -ition -ation -ful -less -ic -an -ian -n -al -ary -y -ance -ant -ence -er -ness -ment -able -ible -en -ous -ure -ity -ly -ive -s -es -d -ed -ing

These affixes may be added to a root word to form another word. Listed below are four words to which an affix has been added. Identify the root word and write it on the first line. Then make five more words by adding a different affix.

A. earnings

root word_____   1._____

2. _____   3. _____

4._____   5._____

B. freshened

root word_____   1. _____

2._____   3. _____

4. _____   5._____

C. fruitful

root word_____   1. _____

2._____   3. _____

4. _____   5._____

D. decidedly

root word_____   1. _____

2._____   3. _____

4. _____   5._____

An affix is any letter or group of letters added to a word. If the affix is at the beginning of the word, it is a *prefix*. If it is added to the end of a word, it is a *suffix*. Below is a list of the most common affixes.

PREFIXES: ab- ad- be- com- de- dis- en- em- in- pre- pro- re- sub- un-
SUFFIXES: -ion -ition -ation -ful -less -ic -an -ian -n -al -ary -y -ance -ant -ence -er -ness -ment -able -ible -en -ous -ure -ity -ly -ive -s -es -d -ed -ing

These affixes may be added to a root word to form another word. Listed below are four words to which an affix has been added. Identify the root word and write it on the first line. Then make five more words by adding a different affix.

A. disconnect

    root word_____   1._____

    2. _____   3. _____

    4._____   5._____

B. assumed

    root word_____   1. _____

    2._____   3. _____

    4. _____   5._____

C. disheartened

    root word_____   1. _____

    2._____   3. _____

    4. _____   5._____

D. exceeding

    root word_____   1. _____

    2._____   3. _____

    4. _____   5._____

An affix is any letter or group of letters added to a word. If the affix is at the beginning of the word, it is a *prefix*. If it is added to the end of a word, it is a *suffix*. Below is a list of the most common affixes.

PREFIXES: ab- ad- be- com- de- dis- en- em- in- pre- pro- re- sub- un-
SUFFIXES: -ion -ition -ation -ful -less -ic -an -ian -n -al -ary -y -ance -ant -ence -er -ness -ment -able -ible -en -ous -ure -ity -ly -ive -s -es -d -ed -ing

These affixes may be added to a root word to form another word. Listed below are four words to which an affix has been added. Identify the root word and write it on the first line. Then make five more words by adding a different affix.

A. laughable

root word_____   1._____

2. _____   3. _____

4._____   5._____

B. recollect

root word_____   1. _____

2._____   3. _____

4. _____   5._____

C. wizened

root word_____   1. _____

2._____   3. _____

4. _____   5._____

D. typist

root word_____   1. _____

2._____   3. _____

4. _____   5._____

An affix is any letter or group of letters added to a word. If the affix is at the beginning of the word, it is a *prefix*. If it is added to the end of a word, it is a *suffix*. Below is a list of the most common affixes.

PREFIXES: ab- ad- be- com- de- dis- en- em- in- pre- pro- re- sub- un-
SUFFIXES: -ion -ition -ation -ful -less -ic -an -ian -n -al -ary -y -ance -ant -ence -er -ness -ment -able -ible -en -ous -ure -ity -ly -ive -s -es -d -ed -ing

These affixes may be added to a root word to form another word. Listed below are four words to which an affix has been added. Identify the root word and write it on the first line. Then make five more words by adding a different affix.

A. stopper

root word_____   1._____

2. _____   3. _____

4._____   5._____

B. shelved

root word_____   1. _____

2._____   3. _____

4. _____   5._____

C. paring

root word_____   1. _____

2._____   3. _____

4. _____   5._____

D. mockingly

root word_____   1. _____

2._____   3. _____

4. _____   5._____

1. Read each word below and write the first definition that comes to mind.

charge _____   counter _____

chief _____   crook _____

coast_____   cross _____

complete _____   current _____

2. These same words have been used in the sentences below. Write a definition for each word as it is used in the sentence. Compare the definition with your first choice.

1. The elephants began to **charge** when they heard the guns.
2. The **chief** reason we are doing the report is because we like the subject.
3. Sally stopped pedaling the bicycle and began to **coast** down the hill.
4. I have a **complete** set of baseball cards.
5. I will **counter** your idea with a new one.
6. The bird built its nest in a **crook** on the bottom limb of the tree.
7. Aunt Sara was **cross** because we broke her window.
8. An electrical **current** runs through that wire so be very careful.

3. Give a definition for the word as it is used in the sentence.

charge_____

chief_____

coast_____

complete_____

counter_____

crook_____

cross_____

current_____

1. Read each word below and write the first definition that comes to mind.

draft _____   fair _____

spell _____   fashion _____

drop_____   flag _____

express _____   fudge _____

2. These same words have been used in the sentences below. Write a definition for each word as it is used in the sentence. Compare the definition with your first choice.

1. This first copy of my paper is only the rough **draft.**
2. I am very tired and need to just sit down for a **spell.**
3. Did I just feel a **drop** of rain?
4. Do you have an **express** flight to New York?
5. The child had **fair** skin and blue eyes.
6. Joan can **fashion** a vase out of old milk bottles.
7. John began to **flag** after running only one mile. He was too tired to finish the race.
8. No one is allowed to **fudge** on this test. If you are caught you will fail it!

3. Give a definition for the word as it is used in the sentence.

draft_____

spell_____

drop_____

express_____

fair_____

fashion_____

flag_____

fudge_____

1. Read each word below and write the first definition that comes to mind.

litter _____   sand _____

long _____   season _____

produce_____   sharp _____

resort _____   staple _____

2. These same words have been used in the sentences below. Write a definition for each word as it is used in the sentence. Compare the definition with your first choice.

1. Our dog just had a **litter** of puppies.
2. I **long** for a cold glass of water because I am so hot and thirsty.
3. You will find fruits and vegetables in the **produce** department at the grocery store.
4. Please do not **resort** to calling me names.
5. **Sand** the wood before you paint it.
6. **Season** the meat with salt before you eat it.
7. Eric is a very **sharp** student. He always gets great grades!
8. Bread is a **staple** food in our house. We have it at every meal.

3. Give a definition for the word as it is used in the sentence.

litter_____

long_____

produce_____

resort_____

sand_____

season_____

sharp_____

staple_____

1. Read each word below and write the first definition that comes to mind.

tense _____   raise _____

toast _____   stage _____

troop_____   steer _____

type _____   stalk _____

2. These same words have been used in the sentences below. Write a definition for each word as it is used in the sentence. Compare the definition with your first choice.

1. Make sure that you use the proper **tense** of the verb.
2. The best man will make the **toast** at the wedding.
3. The class will **troop** to library after lunch.
4. A glass is a **type** of container for water.
5. I don't think I ever want to **raise** children!
6. The first **stage** of the plan is to brainstorm for new ideas.
7. That **steer** with the long horns will be perfect for the rodeo.
8. The thief would **stalk** his victims by following them in his car.

3. Give a definition for the word as it is used in the sentence.

tense_____

toast_____

troop_____

type_____

raise_____

stage_____

steer_____

stalk_____

1. Read each word below and write the first definition that comes to mind.

stem _____   bridge _____
stern _____   brush _____
scrap_____   curry _____
bluff _____   drove _____

2. These same words have been used in the sentences below. Write a definition for each word as it is used in the sentence. Compare the definition with your first choice.

1. We must **stem** this problem before it gets any worse.
2. A flag usually hangs on the **stern** on a ship.
3. Karen got into a **scrap** with her best friend.
4. The artist liked to sit on a **bluff** high above the ocean.
5. My parents like to play **bridge** every Wednesday night.
6. The hunters sat in the **brush** four hours before they saw a deer.
7. You must **curry** the horse with a large brush before you put it in the stall.
8. A **drove** of cattle was crossing the road so we had to stop and wait for them.

3. Give a definition for the word as it is used in the sentence.

stem_____

stern_____

scrap_____

bluff_____

bridge_____

brush_____

curry_____

drove_____

1. Read each word below and write the first definition that comes to mind.

entrance _____   fold _____

fawn _____   fresh _____

fell_____   fuse _____

firm _____   stall _____

2. These same words have been used in the sentences below. Write a definition for each word as it is used in the sentence. Compare the definition with your first choice.

1. The sound of bagpipes can **entrance** many people.
2. I cannot stand it when you **fawn** over me because you want a favor.
3. The villain sneered before he did his **fell** deed.
4. My mother works for a law **firm.**
5. The sheep were in the **fold** for the night.
6. The young child was being **fresh** with his mother so she sent him to his room.
7. We will **fuse** the pieces together so they will not come apart again.
8. The vendor set up his **stall** at the fair so he could sell his goods.

3. Give a definition for the word as it is used in the sentence.

entrance_____

fawn_____

fell_____

firm_____

fold_____

fresh_____

fuse_____

stall_____

1. Read each word below and write the first definition that comes to mind.

grave _____   hold _____

hamper _____   incense _____

hawk_____   jerky _____

heel _____   jet _____

2. These same words have been used in the sentences below. Write a definition for each word as it is used in the sentence. Compare the definition with your first choice.

1. This is a very **grave** matter, and you should not laugh about it.
2. That coat is too long and will **hamper** you when you run.
3. The popcorn vendor began to **hawk** his goods at the circus.
4. The sailboat began to **heel** as the wind blew harder.
5. Sailors store cargo in the **hold** of the ship.
6. Your rude comments **incense** me.
7. Many cowboys ate **jerky** because it would not spoil during long cattle drives.
8. We used a **jet** of air to blow the leaves from the lawn.

3. Give a definition for the word as it is used in the sentence.

grave_____

hamper_____

hawk_____

heel_____

hold_____

incense_____

jerky_____

jet_____

1. Read each word below and write the first definition that comes to mind.

key _____   leave _____

lap _____   line _____

lark_____   list _____

leagues _____   meter _____

2. These same words have been used in the sentences below. Write a definition for each word as it is used in the sentence. Compare the definition with your first choice.

1. The third **key** on the piano is broken.
2. Dogs and cats **lap** water to get a drink.
3. The boys put salt in the sugar bowl just for a **lark.**
4. Submarines can go many **leagues** under the ocean.
5. I give you my **leave** to go to the park with your friends.
6. I will **line** your jacket with flannel so it will be warmer.
7. The ship began to **list** when water poured in through the crack in the side.
8. We needed a new water **meter** so we could measure how much we used each month.

3. Give a definition for the word as it is used in the sentence.

key_____

lap_____

lark_____

leagues_____

leave_____

line_____

list_____

meter_____

1. Read each word below and write the first definition that comes to mind.

nip _____   press _____
pitch _____   quack _____
pine_____   refuse _____
post _____   rifle _____

2. These same words have been used in the sentences below. Write a definition for each word as it is used in the sentence. Compare the definition with your first choice.

1. I would like just a **nip** from your bottle of soda.
2. The workers filled the holes in the road with **pitch.**
3. The puppy began to **pine** for its mother as soon as we took it out of the litter.
4. The guard could not leave his **post** even for a minute.
5. The **press** reported on the hurricane that was headed our way.
6. That doctor is nothing but a **quack.**
7. The garbage collector put the **refuse** in the back of his truck.
8. Joe had to **rifle** through a stack of pictures before he found the one he wanted.

3. Give a definition for the word as it is used in the sentence.

nip_____

pitch_____

pine_____

post_____

press_____

quack_____

refuse_____

rifle_____

1. Read each word below and write the first definition that comes to mind.

shed _____   snarl _____

shock _____   soil _____

shore_____   strain _____

size _____   tart _____

2. These same words have been used in the sentences below. Write a definition for each word as it is used in the sentence. Compare the definition with your first choice.

1. **Shed** those wet clothes before you catch a cold!
2. The child had a **shock** of red hair and freckles.
3. We need to **shore** this porch before it falls down. See how it leans over there?
4. Please **size** this strip of wallpaper so we can hang it.
5. I have quite a **snarl** in my hair
6. Do not **soil** your your best clothes by playing in the mud .
7. There is a new **strain** of the flu going around this year.
8. My grandmother baked a strawberry **tart** for dessert.

3. Give a definition for the word as it is used in the sentence.

shed_____

shock_____

shore_____

size_____

snarl_____

soil_____

strain_____

tart_____

Read the following sentences. Use the context clues to help you decide what the word in boldface means. Circle the definition that you think best fits the word.

Example: We must **abolish** weapons in schools.
             permit   (ban)   allow

1.   Garages are usually **adjacent** to houses.
    inside   next to   over

2.   The empty building was **ablaze** by the time the fire trucks got there.
    full   on fire   torn down

3.   I want to **amend** my last answer on that test. I have more to add to it.
    erase   turn in   improve

4.   Joshua certainly has the **aptitude** for painting. He took first place at the show.
    ability   desire   quickness

5.   I want to **assert** my opinion about the candidate.
    anchor   ban   declare

6.   You will need to change your **attire** to dine there. They don't allow jeans.
    manner of dress   manner of eating   manner of writing

7.   The designer made a **blueprint** of how the room will look when it is finished.
    color   photograph   plan

8.   Joey is a **brawny** lad, which makes him great at football.
    decent   muscular   thin

9.   Matt got his **breeches** wet when he sat too near the pool.
    books   shoes   trousers

10. I will **wager** that Mark wins the race!
    bet   brag   consider

Read the following sentences. Use the context clues to help you decide what the word in boldface means. Circle the definition that you think best fits the word.

Example: We must **abolish** weapons in schools.
            permit   (ban)   allow

1. Susan is **brusque** when she says what she thinks. She doesn't pull any punches!
   blunt   gentle   kind

2. The thieves found a **cache** for the stolen jewels.
   cash   hiding place   pocket

3. I don't mean to be **callous,** but I find it hard to feel sorry for you.
   funny   kind   unfeeling

4. That **canine** is barking and growling at us!
   blister   cat   dog

5. My legs were **chafed** after riding the horse all day.
   longer   rubbed until sore   tired out

6. Larry's mother really **chided** him for missing the school bus this morning.
   helped   laughed at   scolded

7. I don't understand this book. Can you **clarify** a few points for me?
   aide   help with   make clear

8. Helen is a **competent** worker, completing her work carefully.
   capable   confident   likely

9. I will **concede** to your wishes this time, but next time I get to choose.
   deny   fall   grant

10. The collar began to **constrict** around Danny's throat, making it hard to breathe.
    open   squeeze   tempt

Name _____

Skill: vocabulary

Read the following sentences. Use the context clues to help you decide what the word in boldface means. Circle the definition that you think best fits the word.

Example: We must **abolish** weapons in schools.
        permit   (ban)   allow

1.   You need a softer **contour** to that circle. The line is much too straight.
    color   mixture   shape

2.   The puppy **cowered** in the corner when his master yelled at him.
    sat up   snuggled into   shrunk from fear

3.   You are **daft** for suggesting that I drive. I haven't gotten a license yet!
    foolish   happy   honest

4.   I **deem** it necessary to leave the party now.
    celebrate   fear   think

5.   Judy must **despise** that movie. She said no one should go see it.
    adore   hate   love

6.   The hunter pulled a **dirk** from its sheath and quickly cut the rope.
    dagger   can opener   tool

7.   Help me **dismantle** this table so it will fit through the door.
    break   put together   take apart

8.   The nurse **dispensed** the medicine to the patients.
    gave out   held   shot

9.   Gloria was **elated** to hear she won the math contest.
    filled with fear   filled with joy   sad

10. The waves **eroded** the beach until the sand was nearly gone.
    filled up   splashed   wore away

©1995 Kelley Wingate Publications   96   CD-3715

Read the following sentences. Use the context clues to help you decide what the word in boldface means. Circle the definition that you think best fits the word.

Example: We must **abolish** weapons in schools.
          permit   (ban)   allow

1.   That song always **evokes** tears when I hear it.
     brushes away   calls forth   washes

2.   You are very smart and will **excel** in your studies if you try.
     do very well   fail   lag

3.   What is for dinner? I am **famished.**
     in a hurry   starving   tired

4.   The **flora** in the woods is always so green and lush this time of year.
     animals   growing   plants

5.   I think I **fractured** my arm when I fell. Please call a doctor.
     broke   bruised   bumped

6.   Beth acts so **giddy** when she wears a costume. It makes me laugh to watch her.
     grown up   serious   silly

7.   I can't believe you **goaded** me into doing this when I didn't want to!
     asked   scared   urged

8.   I prefer to live in a **hamlet** rather than a big city.
     country   house   small village

9.   A **horde** of bees flew from the nest when Peg hit it with a stick.
     swarm   thick   vast distance

10. Teresa is in a **festive** mood this evening. I think she likes this party.
     dull   serious   joyous

Read the following sentences. Use the context clues to help you decide what the word in boldface means. Circle the definition that you think best fits the word.

Example: We must **abolish** weapons in schools.

              permit   (ban)   allow

1.   You are so smart, it is hard to believe you could make such an **idiotic** statement!
    brilliant   foolish   quiet

2.   This water is **impure** and not fit to drink.
    clear   cold   not pure

3.   The boy stumbled near the puddle so much it was **inevitable** that he would fall in.
    bound to happen   not likely   radiant

4.   The small mound of dirt was **infested** with ants.
    nearly empty   swarming   wasted

5.   I will **inquire** about the departure time for the plane.
    ask   fumble   require

6.   It is a miracle that the vase is still **intact** after falling on this hard floor.
    broken   guarded   undamaged

7.   The sailor turned off the motor and put up the **jib** because the wind began to blow.
    anchor   rope   sail

8.   Water dripped from the dog's **jowls** after he drank thirstily.
    lower jaw   paws   tail

9.   I need to more flour to make this bread. Please get a sack from the **larder** in the kitchen.
    back yard   cellar   pantry

10. Please write your assignment in a **legible** manner so I won't need and interpreter to understand it.
    design   readable   thoughtless

Read the following sentences. Use the context clues to help you decide what the word in boldface means. Circle the definition that you think best fits the word.

Example: We must **abolish** weapons in schools.
           permit   (ban)   allow

1.   Don't play with that chemical because swallowing it is **lethal.**
     deadly   legal   warm

2.   The thought that it will rain on this beautiful sunny day is **ludicrous.**
     happy   ridiculous   smart

3.   The children made a **valiant** effort to clean up that big empty lot, but the job was was too big.
     brave   gentle   timid

4.   If those two companies **merge** they will become the biggest company in the state.
     back down   part ways   unite

5.   The room was filled with the **mirth** of young children during the party.
     boots   joy   sleepiness

6.   Joyce's face was **mottled** when she had the measles.
     creased and wrinkled   marked with spots   tightly drawn

7.   The **wayfarer** looked as if he had come a great distance with that heavy suitcase.
     cab driver   father   traveler

8.   Using gum instead of glue is a **novel** idea!
     fancy   patterned   unusual

9.   That sun bonnet is terribly **outmoded.** Find a better hat to wear.
     dry   old fashioned   pretty

10. I am **parched.** Could I please have a big glass of water?
     angry   starving   very dry

Name _____

Read the following sentences. Use the context clues to help you decide what the word in boldface means. Circle the definition that you think best fits the word.

Example: We must **abolish** weapons in schools.

          permit   (ban)   allow

1. Those flowers will **perish** if you don't put them in water right away.
    bloom   die or spoil   wander

2. The student looked **perplexed** when the teacher spoke in another language.
    happy   nervous   puzzled

3. You can **preserve** your drawing by putting it in a frame with glass.
    keep or save   sketch   watch

4. The **primary** reason for going to school is to learn.
    easiest   first or most important   least likely

5. The broken glass in the road **punctured** the tire.
    blasted   jacked up   made a hole in

6. I will **rebel** if you tell me I have to wash the dishes again tonight.
    disobey   go back to bed   love the idea

7. Sandy **recoiled** when his hand accidentally brushed against the snake.
    considered   drew back   grabbed

8. I can **recollect** a time when bread cost only ten cents a loaf!
    make up   look at   remember

9. James would like to **reform** our plan a little. He has some really good ideas to improve it.
    change   cushion   try it out

10. The smell of that skunk is enough to **repel** even a person with a stuffy nose!
    attract   drive away   odor

Read the following sentences. Use the context clues to help you decide what the word in boldface means. Circle the definition that you think best fits the word.

Example: We must **abolish** weapons in schools.
permit   (ban)   allow

1.   I am tired and need to **repose** myself.
fan   rest   stand up

2.   You have been working for hours. It is time for a **respite.**
bicycle ride   piece of cake   short rest

3.   We will **revere** the memory of this great person for the rest of our lives.
attack   forget   honor

4.   We were **scantily** equipped for such a long trip. We quickly ran out of food.
barely enough   heavily   well

5.   The man was gritting his teeth and his face was dark looking. It was easy to see that he was **seething** about something.
angry   choking   elated

6.   I wondered how the baby could sleep so **serenely** in the middle of the storm.
in a ball   noisily   peacefully

7.   This diamond you bought is a worthless **sham.**
fake   jewel   shape

8.   Mike polished his shoes until they had quite a **sheen** on them.
dark look   shoelace   shine

9.   The boys took the **skiff** across the lake this morning.
kite   small animal   small boat

10. Erin was **sopping** after she stood in the rain for an hour.
very cold   very dry   very wet

Read the following sentences. Use the context clues to help you decide what the word in boldface means. Circle the definition that you think best fits the word.

Example: We must **abolish** weapons in schools.
   permit   (ban)   allow

1. My baby grand piano will fit well in this **spacious** apartment.
   lovely   roomy   well lit

2. Rita showed a lot of **spunk** when she stood up to that bully.
   courage   fear   silliness

3. The rotting onion created a terrible **stench** in the refrigerator.
   fragrance   stain   stink

4. I think two sandwiches each should **suffice.**
   be enough   direct   make hungry

5. The tramp wore **tattered** clothes and there were holes in his shoes.
   ragged   tidy   trim

6. My mother tends to be **testy** when she has a headache.
   available   cranky   mellow

7. Everyone is wearing that kind of shoe these days. It must be a new **trend.**
   current style   development   sneaker

8. The dog had an **uncanny** way of knowing when I was on my way home.
   bent   keen   weird

9. The traveler had not washed or shaved in days, and his clothes were **unkempt.**
   clean   not neat   soggy

10. Don't worry about losing the game. It is a **trivial** matter.
   lasting   unimportant   very important

Answer Key

What Is Communication?

The word communicate means to share or make known. Almost every person in the world communicates with at least one other person every day of his life. In many ways it is easy to see how we communicate. In the classroom we listen to the teacher and other classmates as they talk. Talking and listening are kinds of auditory (listening) and oral (speaking) communication. We engage in auditory communication when we talk with others face-to-face, over the telephone, or as we listen to the radio. Speech is probably the most common form of communication, but it is certainly not the only form.

When we read we are taking part in another form of communication. Someone else has written a message of some sort, some information that we share when we read it. Letters, books, newspapers, and magazines are all types of written communication. Most written communication is visual, or uses the eyes. There is a form of writing that is not visual. Can you guess what it is? A blind person usually knows how to read books and other material. They use a special writing system called braille. Braille is an alphabet that uses raised dots that are punched onto a piece of paper. A person who learns the braille letters can read by feeling the raised letters as they slide their fingertips across them. This written form of communication uses the sense of touch and is called kinesthetic.

Sometimes we may watch a movie or a video in class or after school. Because the film is sharing information with us, this too is a form of communication. Movies, videos, and most filmstrips combine visual and auditory communication. You receive information through use of both your eyes and your ears. Try turning the sound off while watching a movie. It is not nearly as exciting or easy to understand when you receive only half of the intended message. Turn the sound back on, but turn your back until you cannot see the movie. Again, it is difficult to understand the full message. Television, movies, and most computers are forms of audio-visual communication that we are all familiar with.

There is another form of communication that has very little to do with words. Think about a person who is frowning and rubbing their forehead. They are communicating a message that says something is wrong, although they have not said a word. Gestures and actions are nonverbal (not oral) ways to communicate. A hug, smile, or glare sends a message that most people can understand, even if they don't speak the same language as the person sending the message.

When you think about it, there are many forms of communication. Signals are a type of communication and can be made in a variety of ways. Flashes of light, smoke, flags, drums, colors, horns, and guns have all been used to convey (send) messages. Pictures on road signs communicate warnings or other important information to travelers. Some colors and pictures have become international signals that can be

---

recognized by people no matter what language they may speak. For example, the redcircle with a diagonal slash through it means "no" and is used in many different countries. These signals are important forms of communication that warn or help people, no matter where they are.

1. **What is the main idea of this story?**
   (A) Communication is a way of sharing information and can take many forms.
   B. Signals are nonverbal forms of communication.
   C. Television and radio are the most important forms of communication.

2. **What is auditory and oral communication?**
   Listening and speaking

3. **Name three types of visual communication:**
   letters, books, magazines, newspapers

4. **What does the word "kinesthetic" mean?**
   A. a ruler or leader
   B. running the fingertip over raised dots
   (C) using the sense of touch

5. **Explain how different types of communication can be combined to give a more complete message:**
   combine audio and visual for more input see and hear the message

6. **What word means "not spoken aloud"?**
   A. visual
   B. auditory
   (C) nonverbal

7. **Name three types of nonverbal communication:**
   hug, smile, frown, etc.

8. **What are signals?**
   communication using other forms

9. **Name five types of signals:**
   road signs, light, smoke, flag, drum, color horn, gun, etc...

THINK AHEAD: Draw a picture of three symbols that you find in public places. Tell what each one means.

Language

Language is a system of communication where meaningful sounds are produced and heard by the ear. Humans are the only known animals that use language. It is impossible to trace the development of language, but it is believed that humans have used it for at least the past 40,000 years. However language developed, there are somewhere between three and eight thousand different languages spoken around the world today.

Despite the fact that there are so many languages, they all share some common components, or parts. Linguists (people who study languages) agree that languages are fairly similar in organization and function. First, all languages have some form of nouns and verbs. Second, every language puts words together in groups to form sentences that express some thought. And third, every language makes a distinction among statements (I have the book.), questions (Do I have the book?), and commands (Give me the book!).

Most children from any culture learn to speak thier native language quite well by the age of four or five, even if they are not instructed. Young children also have the physical ability to pronounce sounds from other languages quite easily. This ability begins to drop off when children reach the early teen years, making it more difficult to learn a second language. Why this happens is not known, but it holds true for children of all cultures.

Language is one of the important ties that bring us all together. It allows us to express ourselves clearly as well as understand others better. We use it to gather information and to give out information. Language is a wonderful tool that we use in communicating.

1. **What is the main idea of this story?**
   (A) Language is a communication tool.
   B. Different languages can be very similar, sharing common components.
   C. Humans are the only animals that use language.

2. **How did language in humans develop?**
   no one knows

3. **What does the word "linguist" mean?**
   A. complex structure of language
   B. ability to pronounce words at an early age
   (C) a person who studies language

---

4. **What are the three ways that all languages are similar?**
   all have some form of nouns and verbs, all use words in groups to express a thought, all use statements, exclamation and questions

5. **What happens to a child's ability to learn new languages in the early teen years?**
   The ability drops off

6. **About how long has man used language?**
   At least 40,000 years

7. **What are some of the important aspects of language?**
   it brings us all together. It allows us to express ourselves and understand each other. We are able to gather and give out information.

8. **Name some ways we can communiate without speaking.**
   sign language, body gestures, written words, smoke signals etc..

9. **What are some words or phrases you can think of from other languages?**
   bonjour, adios, ciao, aurevior, très bien, muchos gracias,

THINK AHEAD: Name at least three languages that are spoken by the people in your community or area.

Answer Key

Name _____ Skill: comprehension

Calls and Whistles

Perhaps you have seen a movie about early settlers in North America. These settlers could be going through a forest or sitting by a campfire at night when they hear a bird whistle, an owl hoot, or a coyote howl. They sit up, wondering if the call came from an animal or from Indians. These imitations of animal calls were often used by Indians or hunters as a means of communication. A bird call or whistle, if done well enough, might be easily mistaken for the real thing. This allowed the hunters to keep in contact with each other and not alert the prey to the danger they were about to face.

The call of animals native to an area has been used in many parts of the world. The Comanche Indians often imitated coyotes and owls found in the areas where they lived. Some Indians along the Amazon River in South America used the call of the trumpeter bird to signal one another. Other tribes imitated the Brazilian lapwing to sound out warnings of danger. In New Guinea some of the natives would croak like frogs to signal a meeting of several villages.

These signals were very good for communicating at close distances. The wider the spread between the groups, the louder the call had to become. Groups in the Philippine Islands and India preferred to use very loud, shrill cries to communicate with each other over distances. Gomerans off the coast of Africa have developed a whistling language that can be heard from island to island, up to six miles away! Other African communities use baked clay whistles, flutes, or animal horns to send signals. By working out a code for the sounds, people are able to communicate a variety of messages over a distance that the human voice just could not reach.

1. What is the main idea of this story?
   A. Indians used bird calls to communicate while sneaking up on settlers.
   B. All kinds of animals are imitated throughout the world.
   C.Calls and whistles were used to send messages further than a voice could.
2. Why might animal calls be used even when people were close enough to shout to one another?
   so the prey would not realize it was in danger
3. Name five animals that have been imitated as a form of communication:
   coyote, owl, trumpet, bird, frog, lapwing

©1995 Kelley Wingate Publications   7   KW 1018

---

4. What might the sound of a croaking frog mean in New Guinea?
   a village meeting
5. What advantages do calls and whistles have over the human voice?
   they can be heard at greater distances
6. What kind of communication have the Gomerans developed? What is the furthest distance a message can be heard?
   a whistling language about six miles
7. What three instruments or tools do some African tribes use to communicate with distant villages?
   whistles, flutes and animal horns

THINK AHEAD: Describe a situation you might be in where whistles might be more helpful than words.

©1995 Kelley Wingate Publications   8   KW 1018

Name _____ Skill: comprehension

Drums

When we think of a drum we usually think of a musical instrument. Drums are part of almost every musical group, from small trios to huge orchestras. The drum has also been used for centuries as an important means of communication. The human voice is very good for communication, but it has one very big disadvantage: it cannot be heard very far. As early humans began to live in groups and interact with each other they needed a way to communicate with nearby villages. They could send runners from village to village with an important message, but that took a lot of time. It was discovered that beating on hollow logs could be heard for greater distances, and so a new form of communication called "talking drums" was born.

In many primitive (early) communities a large drum was set in the middle of the village to serve as a way of sending messages to nearby tribes. The drums were made of a variety of materials including goatskin, pottery, gourds, or wood. The drums ranged in size from small enough to be held by one person to eighteen feet wide or more! They could be beaten on with hands or sticks, and some produced a sound when they were rubbed. Some of the larger drums could be heard up to sixteen miles away!

The Ashanti of West Africa developed an amazing talking drum system. Their drums were made of round pieces of hollowed out wood that were four to five feet long. A skin (often an elephant ear) was stretched over one end of the wood and was held in place by a rope. The skin was tightened or loosened to produce higher and lower sounds. The Ashanti used two drums at the same time: one that made low tones (called a male) and one that made higher tones (called a female). They had learned to use the drums so well that they could actually imitate the language that they spoke! The drums sounded much like a person speaking in a voice loud enough to be heard over a large distance.

Most systems of drum communication used a series of beats (like Morse Code) that meant something to the trained listener. The messages usually involved a notice of danger, death, war, or other news of great importance. The message could be sent great distances by a sort of relay system. That is, one village would send a message and a nearby village would hear it. They would then repeat the message on their drums, sending it on to their neighbors. Some relay systems worked so well that they could send a message about 200 miles about as quickly as a telegraph could be sent!

Although "talking drums" developed into a pretty good system of communicating over distances, it had one very big disadvantage. Just as drums could be heard by the neighboring villages, they could also be heard by anyone else in the area. If approaching enemies knew how to interpret the drum messages they would know what was being said or even planned by their intended victims. Communication by drums certainly did not offer privacy!

©1995 Kelley Wingate Publications   9   KW 1018

---

1. What is the main idea of this story?
   A. The Ashanti created "talking drums".
   B.Drums have been used as a form of communication.
   C. Drums can be heard over great distances.
2. What advantage do drums have over human voices?
   drums can be heard at greater distances
3. What is the biggest disadvantage of using drums to communicate?
   everyone can hear them — there is no privacy
4. What does the word "primitive" mean?
   A.having to do with early ages
   B. drums used as voices
   C. private
5. What are male and female drums?
   male drums have deep tones female drums have higher tones
6. Describe a drum "relay system":
   a message is sent to a distant village a second village sends it to the next village and so on
7. What were drums used as in primitive communities? What were they made of?
   to send messages to nearby tribes goatskin, pottery, gourds or wood
8. Describe an Ashanti drum.
   made of round pieces of hollowed out wood with a skin stretched over one end and held in place by a rope.
9. Name 5 other forms of communication.
   telephone, telegram, telephone, mail, computer... answers will vary

THINK AHEAD: Create a communication system you could use to send messages from one place to another without using speech.

©1995 Kelley Wingate Publications   10   KW 1018

Answer Key

Body Language and Gestures

People do not always need to use words to communicate with others. Often their body position and gestures tell a lot more than their words do. Sending messages through positions and gestures is called body language. Body language expresses emotions and attitudes. We display how we are feeling even when our words may be saying something else. For example, a classmate tells you that she is not the least bit nervous about taking a test that day. She says she has studied hard and is confident that she will do very well. You don't really believe what she has said, but you don't know exactly why. Without either of you being aware of it, she has been sending silent messages that don't agree with what she is saying. While talking, the girl is twisting a strand of hair round and round one finger. Her eyes are darting nervously about the room and she is jiggling one foot quickly up and down. The girl's body language reveals what she is really feeling!

Researchers have found that certain acts reveal specific meanings. First, head and facial movements tell a lot about what a person is feeling. Heads that are held high send the message of pride. Twitching facial muscles may indicate extreme nervousness or anger. Second, body positions reveal how strong those feelings are. A person leaning forward in a chair is saying he is interested or sincere. Third, the eyes tell a lot about attitudes and changes in feelings. For example, avoiding direct eye contact often sends the message that the person does not feel comfortable talking in that situation. When a person is excited or interested the pupils of the eyes will dilate, or open wider.

Gestures are another form of body language that can send messages to other people. In Japan, people may greet each other with a bow to show their respect. In Tibet, a person may show respect by sticking out his tongue! Many people clap to show that they appreciate something they have just witnessed. In many cultures people also clap as a way of saying "Thank you". In China you may be regarded as disrespectful if you hand something to another person using only one hand. The object should be handed over with two hands, not one. Hugging, kissing, or pinching cheeks are common forms of greeting in some cultures. In other places these greetings are considered offensive and disrespectful.

Understanding body language and the meaning of gestures can be a full time job! There have been many books written on these topics because it is interesting and can even be helpful. Some employers are trained to become aware of body language to help them learn more about the attitudes of the people they interview for jobs. Politicians and actors are very aware of their body language because it really affects their image in public. Lawyers may use knowledge of body language to help their clients send the appropriate message to the jury. What does your body language say about you?

1. **What is the main idea of this story?**
   A. Body language and gestures can send messages that are stronger than words. *(circled)*
   B. Body language is different all over the world.
   C. Body language and gestures are not forms of communication.

2. **What is body language?**
   body positions that express feelings

3. **Are most people aware of body language? Explain why or why not.**
   No. They don't think about it — they just react naturally

4. **What movements tell a lot about what a person is feeling?**
   head and facial movements

5. **What do body positions tell about a person?**
   What he is really feeling

6. **When a person will not look you in the eye when you are talking, what does that mean?**
   that he is uncomfortable

7. **What word means "to open wider"?**
   A. body language
   B. twitching
   C. dilate *(circled)*

8. **What is the difference between body language and gestures?**
   body language is the position of the body gestures are intentional motions

9. **What is one way of showing that you appreciate something you have just witnessed?**
   clapping

THINK AHEAD: Make a list of eight gestures that have a specific meaning in your culture.

Pictures

Long before man could write he was painting pictures to communicate messages. Pictures carved on the walls of caves have been found throughout the world and can date back 15 to 25 thousand years. Many of these pictures were found deep in caves where there is no light. The artist had to paint by the light of burning moss or melted fat. We know that because a lot of these "lamps" have been found in the caves near the paintings. Each of these pictures tells a story of life long ago. They are still sending messages thousands of years after they were drawn!

Paintings were created by smearing the color on with fingers or a brush. They were usually done in only one or two colors (mainly using yellow, red, black, brown, or white). The Bushmen of Africa were very busy artists. They painted pictures that depict (or describe) animals, hunting methods, weapons, household items, customs, ceremonies, and warfare. The Bushmen used a wide variety of colors - red, orange, yellow, black, and white were most commonly used. Paintings such as these help us trace history and see how people used to live.

Most primitive art was not made by painting. More often the picture was made by etching, or carving, the stone. These ancient carvings are called petroglyphs (Greek for rock carving). Petroglyphs have been found on every continent! They were produced in many different ways. Some petroglyphs were made by rubbing or scratching with a hard stone or tool. Others were chiseled, using a small sharp stone and hitting it with a bigger stone. If you have ever tried to carve your initials on a stone you will know that making petroglyphs was not an easy task!

Pictures are more likely to be found in caves where they are protected from the weather. Petroglyphs, on the other hand, can be found almost any place where there is smooth rock. They can be found all over North and South America, Africa, Australia, and parts of Europe and Asia. You will not find many petroglyphs in the jungles, because most of the rocks there are covered with plants which makes it difficult to find a spot on which to carve.

Many areas where paintings or petroglyphs have been found were made into national monuments or taken to museums in an effort to preserve, or save, them. Many books and magazine articles have discussed these drawings and presented ideas as to what they mean. However, scientists and archaeologists can only guess at their true meaning. It is believed that many of the pictures were connected with religious groups or certain ceremonial rituals. Other pictures may have simply been a way to record important events in the lives of the people who drew them.

The art of cave drawing and rock carving may seem primitive but some modern art is still exhibited in the same way. Graffiti is common on the walls in most major cities and can also be found in rocky areas. Our methods of creating the paintings

have changed (we often use spray paint or metal tools) but the purpose is still a means of expression. What will the scientists of the future think when they uncover our petroglyphs and "wall paintings"?

1. **What is the main idea of this story?**
   A. Ancient cave drawings can be found throughout the world.
   B. Petroglyphs are rock carvings.
   C. The practice of drawing messages or stories in public places is thousands of years old. *(circled)*

2. **How did ancient cave artists provide light so they could see in these dark places?**
   they burned moss or melted fat

3. **What were the most common colors used in cave painting?**
   yellow, brown, black, red, white

4. **What does the word "depict" mean?**
   A. rock carving
   B. represent or describe *(circled)*
   C. early descriptions of hunting

5. **What is the difference between a painting and a petroglyph?**
   a painting uses color painted on a petroglyph is carved on the stone

6. **Which word means "to save or keep safe"?**
   A. petroglyph
   B. etching
   C. preserve *(circled)*

7. **What do scientists believe most of this ancient art was used for?**
   mainly religious ceremonies or recording important events

THINK AHEAD: What forms of modern "cave art" have you seen? What do you think it meant?

Answer Key

Name _____   Skill: comprehension

Writing

Writing is a relatively new invention, dating back only 5,000 years or so. It is not known who invented writing, or exactly when it was created. Scientists do believe that it developed somewhere in Mesopotamia, the land between the Tigris and Euphrates Rivers (what we now call Iraq). The reason we believe this is because archaeologists found clay tablets there, the earliest example of writing ever to be discovered. People called Sumerians lived in that area 5,000 years ago. They were highly civilized, living in cities with temples, businesses, and even banks. The Sumerians developed a sense of personal property, things belonging to an individual instead of a group. It became important to identify who owned which animals, tools, and land. At this time people began to mark their belongings with a personal picture or symbol. They often put their mark on a stone cylinder which they could press into a piece of soft clay or wax. This was the first time pictures began to stand for words.

This stage of development was fairly easy at first. A picture of a cow could represent a cow, a sheep stood for a sheep, and so on. Pictures were good for concrete, or real thing, but pictures could not represent ideas such as sorrow, old, or eat. The Sumerians began to combine pictures to try to represent ideas. For example, an eye with tears falling from it might be used to stand for sorrow. Combining pictures to represent ideas is called ideographs. This was the second stage in writing. The biggest problem with ideographs was that pictures might be interpreted differently by different people. The limits of this system pushed the development to a third, very important, stage.

The Sumerians realized that ideographs could be used to represent sounds as well as objects. A modern example would be a picture of a bee and a leaf. The two pictures as objects mean very little, but the sounds put together give us the word belief. This was the beginning of writing based on phonics, or sounds. Over the years the pictures were changed into marks that were easier to write. These marks were eventually developed into alphabets, symbols representing the smallest unit of meaningful sound. Records and messages could now be written, no matter what idea the writer wanted to express.

Clay was plentiful in Mesopotamia. It could be scooped up almost anywhere along the riverbanks. Clay could also be flattened out and smoothed, making it an excellent place to write. The Sumerians used these clay writing tablets for the next two or three thousand years! The earliest tablets show that the scribes, or people who could write, recorded information in vertical columns beginning at the upper right corner. They wrote down the column to the bottom of the tablet then moved left and back to the top. This system was not used for long, however. Perhaps the scribes became frustrated with having their hand smudge the words as they moved to the left

©1995 Kelley Wingate Publications   15   KW 1018

---

column. Think about writing from right to left: your hand drags over the words you have just written. At any rate, before long it became the custom to begin at the top left and write across the tablet, as most people do today.

1. What is the main idea of this story?
(A) Writing was developed in Mesopotamia about 5,000 years ago.
B. Writing began with pictures representing objects.
C. The Sumerians were highly civilized people.

2. Where is the land that was once called Mesopotamia?
the land now called Iraq — the land between the Tigris and Euphrates Rivers

3. Why did the Sumerians have a need for writing?
to keep track of personal belongings

4. What does the word "concrete" mean as it is used in the story?
A. a hard stone-like material
(B) real or able to be touched
C. the smallest unit of meaningful sound

5. What symbols were used during the second stage of writing development?
Ideographs combined pictures to express abstract ideas

6. What does the word "phonics" mean?
A. alphabetical
B. ideographs
(C) the smallest unit of sound

7. What were scribes?
People who could write

8. What was so important about representing sounds rather than objects?
with sounds instead of entire words, any idea could be represented

THINK AHEAD: Think of at least three examples of words that can be written ideographically. Draw them in picture form.

©1995 Kelley Wingate Publications   16   KW 1018

Name _____   Skill: comprehension

Sign Language

Speaking and writing are wonderful ways to communicate. What happens, however, when two people who speak different languages try to talk with each other? How can the deaf communicate if they cannot hear what is being said? Sign language is a way of communicating without voices that can be used in a variety of situations.

The most widely used sign languages are those used by the deaf. For hundreds of years people who could not hear have used gestures to express themselves. In the mid 1700's a man in France began the first school for the deaf. The common signs used by these people became the basis for an entire non-verbal language system. The signs represent letters, words, or word groups that are put into the sentence structure of the verbal language being signed.

A different form of signing was developed by the Plains Indians so they could communicate with tribes that spoke other languages. Gestures were developed to represent a small vocabulary important to those tribes. Signs for complex ideas were not needed because the Indians had a fairly common background and could also use their verbal language.

1. What is the main idea of this story?
(A) Sign language is a nonverbal way to communicate.
B. Sign language is difficult to learn.
C. The Plains Indians developed a simple sign language.

2. What contributed to the need for developing a sign language?
people speaking different languages needed to communicate

3. Who developed the most commonly used sign language?
deaf people

4. What three parts of language can signs represent?
letters, words and word groups

5. Which Indians developed a form of sign language?
the Plains Indians

6. Why wasn't Indian sign language as complex as sign language for the deaf?
Indians had verbal language to help them — the deaf people did not

THINK AHEAD: In what other ways is sign language used? (Hint: Think of sports!)

©1995 Kelley Wingate Publications   17   KW 1018

Name _____   Skill: comprehension

Braille

For hundreds of years people who were blind or had poor vision had no way to read. They had to rely on verbal communication for most of their learning experiences. In 1829 a man named Louis Braille invented a new system of communication for the blind. He developed an alphabet, numbers, and punctuation marks made up of dots. Different combinations using one to six dots represented different letters, numbers, or letter groups. These dots were pressed into a piece of paper or other flat surface. By lightly running the tips of the fingers across the dots a person was able to read with their hands.

Braille was not widely accepted at first, but by 1932 a standard Braille system for people who spoke English had been instituted, or established, and was used in many schools. Books printed in Braille were now available to people with visual problems. For a number of years Braille has been taught in schools for the blind and visually impaired.

Today tape recorders and computers have made it easier for blind people to learn. There are even machines that can translate (change) the spoken word into print. A visually impaired person can write a letter simply by speaking to the computer! This new technology has created some new problems, however. Blind people who have not learned Braille are finding it very difficult to get good jobs without this skill. It is comparable to a sighted person not being able to read. Use of the television or verbal computer programs is not enough to function at work on an affective level. A few states have laws requiring that Braille be taught to all blind people that are capable of learning it.

1. What is the main idea of this story?
(A) Braille is an important means of communication for people with visual impairments.
B. Braille is a system of dots that can be read with the fingertips.
C. Louis Braille invented Braille in 1829.

2. What is Braille?
a form of writing using raised dots that can be read with fingertips

3. How do the blind use their hands when reading Braille?
by lightly running the tips of their fingers across the dots

©1995 Kelley Wingate Publications   18   KW 1018

Answer Key

---

4. Where was Braille commonly taught after 1932?

mainly in schools for the blind

5. What does the word "translate" mean?
   A. to type Braille
   B. to change from one language to another
   C. to read Braille

6. What has caused people to stop using Braille?

tape recorders and computers that talk made communication easier

7. Why is it important for the blind to learn Braille?

without this skill, it would be difficult for a blind person to get a good job

8. What did blind people rely on for most of their learning experiences before Braille was developed?

verbal communication

9. What are some modern ways that blind people learn other than by reading Braille?

tape recorders and computers

THINK AHEAD: Write a short paragraph describing how your life would be changed if you were suddenly blind. Do you think you would try to learn Braille? Why or why not?

Name _____   Skill: comprehension

Telegraph

For most of the history of man, communication could be transmitted (sent) in two ways: sight and sound. Sight signals were sent by things such as fires, smoke, or light. Bells, whistles, drums, and the human voice were common forms of communication by sound. During the early 1800's, the world was growing rapidly and the need for a fast system of long distance communication was in demand. The discovery of controlled electricity opened the door to that kind of system.

The world was beginning to work with electricity and began to understand it a little better. People quickly realized that it had great power and were interested in finding ways to use it. When it was discovered that electricity could travel over great distances through a tiny wire it was only natural that scientists and inventors thought to apply it to long distance communication. Many people experimented with the idea, so it is not surprising that the first telegraph was not a quick invention thought up by one man. Rather, it was the result of a series of experiments by a number of men, each making a little more progress than the last.

The early telegraph was a very simple machine. It was discovered that an electrical current could be sent through a wire for great distances. It was discovered that when a switch or a key was connected to one end, a person could send a series of short pulses through the wire. The only problem was that no one had figured out a way to receive the pulses at the other end of the line. This problem was solved in 1819 when Hans Oersted discovered that a magnetic needle would react to the electrified wire. These telegraphs became known as electric telegraphs.

In 1831 Samuel Morse devised, or invented, a receiver that would produce a clicking sound when attached to an electric wire. Morse also invented a coding system of dots and dashes that worked really well with the clicking receiver. In 1844 Morse demonstrated this new telegraph by successfully sending a message from Baltimore, Maryland to Washington, D.C. for a group of politicians. Morse's receiver became very popular and was widely adopted. The coding system was easy to learn and could be plainly understood on the clicking telegraph. The system was named after Samuel Morse (Morse Code) and is still used in some situations today.

1. What is the main idea of this story?
   A. Samuel Morse invented the electric telegraph.
   B. Early telegraphs were simple machines.
   C. The telegraph is a way to communicate using electricity and a code of dots and dashes.
2. Before electricity was used, what were the only two ways to send messages?

sight and sound

---

3. How did the discovery of electricity affect our systems of communication?

we could send messages quickly over greater distances

4. What was the problem with early telegraph machines?

no one had figured out a way to receive the pulses at the other end of the line

5. What did Hans Oersted discover in 1819?

that a magnetic needle would react to the electrified wire

6. What does the word "transmit" mean?
   A. to invent
   B. to click out in code
   C. to send

7. What was used as the first receiver for the telegraph?

magnetic needle

8. Who invented a "clicking" receiver and a communication coding system?

Samuel Morse

9. What word means "to invent"?
   A. transmit
   B. devise
   C. code

10. Why did Morse Code become accepted so quickly?

it was easy to learn and could be plainly understood

THINK AHEAD: Find out more about Morse Code by looking in the encyclopedia or other reference book. Write a short message using Morse Code.

Name _____   Skill: comprehension

Telephone

In 1875 Alexander Graham Bell was very interested in the communication problems of the hearing impaired. Bell taught in a school for the deaf, intent on teaching the students how to speak clearly enough to be understood. Because of this interest, Bell invented a machine, the phonautograph, that could record the human voice. Deaf students would speak into this machine as a pencil recorded their speech on a piece of paper. Bell believed that the deaf students could compare the penciled speech patterns with normal speech patterns and correct themselves. His work was successful enough to gain nationwide attention.

Other people who saw Bell's phonautograph saw its potential as a communication device, a way to send the human voice. They encouraged Bell to experiment with the machine, but he was not sure because he knew nothing about electricity. Bell got an assistant, Thomas Watson, who had worked quite a bit with electrical inventions. Bell and Watson tried many experiments with transmitters and receivers and on March 10, 1876 they finally found a way to make the first telephone work.

The telephone was first used in several Boston banks as security systems. The transmitters were installed in the banks and left on all night while a private detective agency listened for intruders. The idea caught on and before long businessmen began to use the telephone as a quick means of communicating among themselves. Within one year of its discovery, the telephone system had been successfully used in Boston and New Haven. Although these systems were fairly small, Bell was ready to open his invention to the world.

By 1888 the telephone had become commonplace in the businesses of large cities. Wires were strung on poles and could be seen throughout the cities and crossing the countryside between cities. The wires created new problems. It took many wires to service the demand for telephones. Soon the poles were thick with telephone lines. During a fire, firemen often had to cut through wires to reach the buildings with their ladders. Heavy snow or ice storms usually snapped wires and caused problems with communications. The problem of hanging wires was eventually solved when they were bundled into cables and buried underground.

As the telephone became common in more and more homes, the system went through many changes as it struggled to keep up with the increase of users. It was clear that even the heavy underground cables could not supply enough circuits to meet the demand. Because all calls had to go through an operator, the telephone exchange companies rapidly grew, but they still could not keep up with the number of calls to be handled. People enjoyed the advantages of having a telephone, and they wanted the service to be faster and easier.

Bell's little business had expanded into a huge company. Its engineers

---

Answer Key

experimented with different ways to improve the system and solve new problems. The dial was invented, allowing customers to call someone directly and not have to speak with an operator. The dial has rapidly given way to push button telephones, an even faster way to "dial" a number. The heavy underground cables have been replaced with flexible glass tubes able to carry many times more circuits than the old wires. Telephones are in nearly every home in North America. Thanks to the invention of portable phones, we can even take them with us when we leave the house! Bell's simple invention to help deaf children has evolved into one of the most important communication systems in the world today.

1. What is the main idea of this story?
    A. Alexander Graham Bell taught deaf children.
    (B) The telephone has become a very important communication tool.
    C. Early telephones created many new problems for cities.

2. Why did Bell become interested in recording the human voice?
he thought it would be easier for the deaf to learn to speak when they could "see" the voice

3. What was the "phonautograph"?
    A. an autograph given by telephone
    B. the first phonograph
    (C) a machine that could record voices

4. Why did Bell choose Thomas Watson as his assistant?
Watson knew about electricity, Bell did not

5. In what uncommon way did the Boston banks first use the telephone?
as a security system

6. What problems did telephone wires create?
they blocked access to buildings; snow pulled down lines; they were ugly to look at

7. How did the invention of the telephone dial improve communication?
it was faster and did not need an operator

THINK AHEAD: Keep a record of telephone calls for one day. Keep track of the number of local and long distance calls. How many calls are for business? For pleasure? How many different ways is your phone used to communicate?

Name _____   Skill: comprehension

What is Conservation?

What happens when you use your last sheet of paper? You, of course, go to the store and buy some more. Pretend that the pack of paper you buy is the last one in the world. Would you waste sheets carelessly, or would you use them only when necessary? What would you do when you ran out again? This may seem like a silly problem because we are talking about plain old paper, but did you know that paper is made from trees? We rely on trees for many other important things such as producing food, providing shade, and even cleaning the air we breathe. If the world ran out of paper it would probably be because there were only enough trees left to provide the more important things we need. The world is not running out of paper, so don't get upset yet, but this problem could happen one day.

During the history of man the earth has seemed like a huge place that was full of resources, or available natural materials. The world population was not very big and the earth was able to produce more materials than man could use. People did not think twice about digging holes to look for gold or chopping down trees to build homes. The supply of natural resources was vast, seeming to have no end. The discovery of two new continents in the 1700's reinforced (supported) the idea of endlessness. These continents were huge land masses full of furs, trees, ore, and other materials people wanted. Few people imagined that the land would ever run out of anything!

During the 1800's the need for lumber was important as the world population increased and many new cities were built. North America was covered with large forests and was a rich source for much of the needed wood. Logging became a booming business with many acres being cleared each day. Forests that had taken hundreds of years to grow were gone within a few years. People began to realize that it would take hundreds of years to replace these forests and, for the first time, they began to worry. Was it possible that man could "use up" the natural resources?

By the late 1800's groups began to organize and plan ways to conserve, or use wisely, our natural resources. They realized that everything on the earth has a limit, and that wasting resources could bring us to the end very quickly. Humans could not stop using wood, for example, but they could control how much was used and what was being done to replace it for the future. Rules and laws were made about the use of forests, soil, and certain wildlife. The world came to understand that we must take care of the earth if we expected the earth to provide for our future needs.

Today, conservation is more than a plan to save trees or animals. It has become a management system for the total environment (everything around us). Scientists have discovered how nature is interrelated, or how each living thing relies on other living things for its survival. Every plant and animal has a purpose and if it is taken away, the absence affects everything else in one way or another. For example, no one

---

is very fond of mosquitoes. At times, almost everyone has wished that there were no mosquitoes! What would happen if they were all destroyed? We might be happy for a while, but soon we would notice a big change. Many small animals that eat mosquitoes, like birds and frogs, would starve. The larger animals that fed on these smaller animals would have less food and would begin to die out. Before long even man would feel the affects by having less available food for himself.

Today, conservationists consider everything in nature and weigh it against the needs of people. We need to use materials from the earth, but we cannot afford to waste them. We are now worried about how things like water and air are used because we realize that the supply is not unlimited. Conservation serves as a balance between what we have to use and what we should not use.

1. What is the main idea of this story?
    (A) Conservation of natural resources is important to the future survival of humans.
    B. Loggers cut down too many trees and wasted lumber.
    C. Everything on the earth is important.

2. Why did people once believe that resources were unlimited?
the world seemed so big and the population seemed so small

3. When did people really begin to realize that there was a need to conserve our natural resources?
During the 1800's, the logging industries cleared acres of land without replacing the trees

4. What does the word "reinforce" mean?
    A. conserve natural resources
    (B) strengthen or support
    C. everything around us

5. Why is every part of the environment important to our survival?
the removal of anything affects some population and, ultimately, man

6. How can the conservation of today help people in the future?
by saving or replacing what we use, it will be around for future generations

THINK AHEAD: List four resources (animals or materials) that are being wasted or destroyed. How might the loss of these resources affect you?

Name _____   Skill: comprehension

Soil Erosion

"That thing is as useless as dirt!" This saying tells a lot about what we think of dirt. We walk on it and dig in it, but we don't really use it for anything important, do we? Think again. Soil is very important to the survival of humans. We grow plants in soil. We find necessary minerals in soil. It truly is an important resource that we must protect. You might ask, "How in the world can you misuse soil?" This is a good question and here is a good answer.

Dirt is full of minerals that are necessary to grow plants. Farmers have learned that adding minerals to the dirt can help produce healthier crops. They have also learned that you cannot grow the same crop in the same field year after year. For example, a crop like corn requires specific minerals to grow. Each year corn is planted, the crop uses more of that mineral. After two or three years that mineral is no longer plentiful and the corn plants begin to suffer. Agricultural (farming) specialists have discovered that crops should be rotated, or changed, from year to year. Planting a crop that requires a different mineral allows the soil to replenish, or restock, the minerals that were used the year before.

Some forms of mining can also hurt the soil. Coal was once a very important source of power. As the demand for coal grew, many mines were established. Tunneling into the earth took a long time and was dangerous work. Coal could not be dug out fast enough to supply the demand. Someone discovered that when coal deposits were fairly close to the surface of the earth it was possible to "strip" the earth away without tunneling (sort of like peeling an orange). Strip mining became very common, tearing up thousands of acres of land each year. When the coal had been mined the stripped land was useless for growing crops.

Erosion, or gradually wearing away, is another problem for soil. Wind blows across the land, often lifting bits of topsoil and carrying it away. Heavy rains and floods flow over the land, pushing and carrying loose soil with it. Wind and water are the two biggest causes of soil erosion. How can we stop the wind from blowing or the rain from falling? We cannot, of course, but we can stop the soil from eroding. Agricultural specialists have found that plants help to keep soil where it belongs. Rows of trees planted around a field help to break the wind so it doesn't carry off the rich topsoil. Proper irrigation (watering) and draining of fields can help to keep water from carrying away large amounts of soil.

Soil is an important resource that we must protect if we want to keep growing food. Now, if you ever hear someone use the expression, "it is as useless as dirt", you will be able to tell them that dirt is far from useless!

Answer Key

Name _____
Skill: comprehension

1. What is the main idea of this story?
   (A) Soil is an important natural resource that needs to be properly conserved.
   B. The saying "useless as dirt" is not true.
   C. Strip mining and crops are harmful to the topsoil.
2. Another word for agricultural is:
   A. peeling
   (B) farming
   C. tunneling
3. Why is soil an important resource?
   we grow plants in soil
   we find necessary minerals in soil
4. Why should crops be rotated every two or three years?
   because each year a crop is planted, it uses
   more minerals —
5. What is strip mining?
   digging up the earth in strips rather
   than tunneling
6. What does the word "replenish" mean?
   A. to remove the upper layer of soil
   (B) to refill or restock
   C. to gradually wear away
7. What are the two biggest causes of soil erosion?
   wind and water
8. What can people do to prevent soil erosion?
   do not leave fields empty of plants; plant
   trees as windbreaks; properly irrigate

THINK AHEAD: Look up the Dust Bowl in the encyclopedia. What did it have to do with soil erosion?

©1995 Kelley Wingate Publications   27   KW 1018

Name _____   Skill: comprehension

Land

The world's population is increasing at a rapid rate. More people means that we need more land to grow the crops that supply food. At the same time, more people means a need for more land to live on. Some scientists believe that the world population will eventually be much larger than our food production and widespread famine (food shortage) will occur. Other authorities believe that we can prevent this from happening if appropriate government policies, research, and technology are used.

Agriculture depends on arable land (land that is suitable for growing crops). The world has about three billion acres of arable land. Currently, less than half of it is being used for farming and we lose millions of acres of it each year. There are several reasons that this arable land is not in use, or disappearing. First, much of this arable land is not ready for production. The largest areas of unused arable land are in Africa. Huge amounts of money will be needed to clear the land, level it, put in irrigation systems, and control for diseases. Second, about 2.5 million acres are lost each year because of improper land management. Much of the arable land is being deforested (cut for timber) or overgrazed by animals. The loss of vegetation, or plant cover is causing erosion. There is a possibility that the land could become desert before it can be saved. Third, about 1.5 million acres of arable land is lost each year as new homes and businesses are built on it.

1. What is the main idea of this story?
   (A) The world is losing millions of acres of arable land each year.
   B. Countries are trying to save their land for farming.
   C. Much of our land is eroding and turning into desert.
2. Why do some scientists predict a famine in the future?
   they feel that the world population will be
   larger than our food production
3. What does the word "arable" mean?
   A. deforested
   B. covered with plants
   (C) suitable for farming
4. Name two reasons that we lose so much arable land each year.
   land is being deforested or built on

THINK AHEAD: Outline a plan to provide housing for the growing world population without using any more of the arable land.

©1995 Kelley Wingate Publications   28   KW 1018

Name _____   Skill: comprehension

Rain Forests

Tropical rainforests (also known as jungles) grow in warm wet regions and can be found in Central and South America, Africa, and Southeast Asia. They are called rainforests because of the heavy amount of rain that falls year round (80 to 160 inches annually). Because it has a warm moist climate, the rainforest is a kind of "hothouse" where plants can grow all year long. Rainforests are thick with vegetation, supporting more than half of all known types of plants in the world. The variety of vegetation helps to support thousands of animal species. For example, a scientist exploring just 2.5 acres of rainforest will find over 200 kinds of trees and plants!

Rainforests are dark and mysterious places that have not been fully explored. They take up less than eight percent of the earth, but more than half of all plant and animal species live there. The thick growth makes it difficult to get very far into the jungle. Most exploration must be done on foot or, in some areas, by boat. Large portions of the rainforests have not been explored yet. It is believed that there are many plants and animals in these areas that have not yet been discovered!

Rainforests also support over half of the known animal species of the world. Recently a scientist conducted research in the rainforests of Panama and Peru. He has estimated that there may be over 30 million species of insects alone in the rainforests! You can also find most reptile, amphibian, and tree dwelling species of animals living within a rainforest. The variety of animals found there number in the thousands.

Tropical rainforests are a rich source of food, medicine, and other useful products. Chocolate, banana, pineapple, and avocado are a few of the foods that originated in these jungles. One out of every four drug prescriptions we use are made from plants that grow in rainforests. Scientists believe that the remedy for such diseases as cancer and heart disease may be found in the plants that grow in the jungle. Many of the plants from the rainforest supply us with products that are a part of our daily lives including chicle (the base for gum), rubber, and cinnamon.

The rainforests are important to the world in many ways. Some of the undiscovered plants and animals may hold the answer to problems of hunger and disease that some of the world now faces. It is impossible to know for certain until the rainforests have been fully explored. One thing we do know at this time is that rainforests are an important part of the world ecology (balance of nature). However, about 30,000 square miles of rainforest are burned or cut down each year. The land is then used for ranching, farming, or industry. It is estimated that 1,000 species of plants and animals are eradicated, or become extinct, each year due to the loss of rainforests. Five out of six species that are destroyed have never been seen by scientists!

©1995 Kelley Wingate Publications   29   KW 1018

Many people understand the importance of preserving, or saving, the rainforests. There are several groups that are active in trying to stop the destruction of these valuable resources. National parks and reserves can be found in most tropical areas. Local farmers are being taught how to produce crops without destroying the rainforest. Through these efforts, perhaps we can save the rainforests which give us so much.

1. What is the main idea of this story?
   a. Chewing gum is made from a tropical plant.
   b. Rainforests are being destroyed.
   (c) Rainforests are an important part of the world ecological system.
2. Why are rainforests a great place for plants to grow?
   the heavy rainfall and warm tempera-
   tures act as a hothouse
3. How many types of trees can typically be found in a 2.5 acre jungle?
   200
4. Name four products we use that come from the rainforest:
   chocolate, bananas, pineapples
   and avocados
5. What does the word "eradicate" mean?
   (a) to wipe out or destroy
   b. to cut down or burn
   c. to save
6. Why are scientists concerned about losing so many acres of rainforest each year?
   we are losing important plants and
   animals that affect other popula-
   tions
7. What word means "to save from destruction"?
   a. ecology
   b. eradicate
   (c) preserve

THINK AHEAD: What might happen to the world if deforesting is allowed to continue?

©1995 Kelley Wingate Publications   30   KW 1018

Answer Key

Name _____ Skill: comprehension

Water

Water is one of our most important natural resources. It is essential (necessary) to all living things. At first glance, the earth's water sources seem limitless. Two-thirds of our planet is covered with water. The oceans and seas contain salt water while lakes, rivers, and ponds contain fresh water. It is used for transportation, irrigation, and recreation. Water also supplies much of our sources of food and energy. Dams are built on rivers to supply power for electricity and reservoirs, or water storage areas, for recreation and wildlife.

Using the water to satisfy human needs is necessary and a good thing. Unfortunately, many ways in which we use the water create waste products, or pollution, that can poison our water supply. Four major causes of water pollution are human waste, factory waste, farm byproducts, and dumping trash.

For many years water has been used as a place to dump unwanted materials. City sewerage systems often got rid of untreated human waste by draining it into nearby water supplies. Although rules and laws were made to stop this from happening, it continues to be a problem in many parts of the world.

Factories produce many products that are necessary to our everyday lives. However, they also produce waste products that must be removed. For many years factories found that the easiest and cheapest way to get rid of their waste was to dump it into rivers and seas. They thought the waste would disappear, or be absorbed back into the water, dirt, or air. We now know that most waste products are not absorbed and do not disappear at all. Instead, they remain in the water and create a danger for animals and humans.

Farmers lose part of their crops to insect pests every year. One way to control this is to spray the crops with chemicals called pesticides. These chemicals kill the insects that destroy their crops and are very helpful in keeping our food supply stable. However, these chemicals do not disappear once they have done their job. They are usually washed into the soil by rain and can find their way into groundwater supplies (pools of water under the soil) that are used as drinking water for nearby towns and cities. Drinking water supplies must now be treated for chemicals such as these pesticides before the water can be piped to homes and businesses.

Each day large cities produce tons of rubbish and trash. One solution to getting rid of trash is to bury it in places called dumps. It has been discovered that chemicals and liquid from this rotting trash can leak into the surrounding groundwater, much as the pesticides do. A second solution commonly used today is to load the trash on barges and dump it into the ocean far off shore. We know that the ocean will not dissolve and absorb the trash, but many people argue that the ocean is very big and a little trash will not seriously harm it.

©1995 Kelley Wingate Publications   31   KW 1018

As more and more of our "unlimited" water supply becomes polluted, people are doing things to help. Laws have been passed to prevent dumping all waste products in or near our water supplies and oceans. Many countries are launching projects aimed at cleaning up polluted rivers and lakes. Others are trying to make everyone aware that we do have a problem and it is time to do something about it.

1. What is the main idea of this story?
   A. Cities are dumping waste into the water.
   B. Factories are a major cause of water pollution.
   C. Water pollution has become a big problem.

2. What are some of the ways we use water?
   transportation, irrigation, recreation

3. What is pollution?
   waste products

4. Name the four major causes of water pollution discussed in this article:
   human waste, factory waste, farm byproducts, dumping trash

5. What does the word "pesticide" mean?
   A. a chemical used to kill insect pests
   B. a form of pollution
   C. absorption of chemicals into the soil

6. In what two ways do people usually get rid of trash or rubbish?
   they bury it or dump it into the ocean

7. What did people believe would happen to the waste dumped into rivers?
   they thought the water would absorb it

8. What things are people doing to prevent water pollution?
   passing laws to prevent pollution, cleaning up polluted areas ...

THINK AHEAD: What does your community do to prevent water pollution?

©1995 Kelley Wingate Publications   32   KW 1018

Name _____ Skill: comprehension

Smog

Nothing is more essential to human life than the air we breathe. Without air, a person will die within minutes. Despite this fact, the very air we breathe is constantly being polluted. Many of the things that help us live more comfortably are major causes of air pollution - power and heat generators, burning solid wastes, industries, and transportation. Small particles of waste turned loose in the air help create dirty clouds commonly known as smog, which has affected more people than any other type of air pollution.

Smog usually occurs in cities where the concentration of air pollution is higher than in rural areas. Smoke in the air provides particles on which water vapor will condense, creating a combination of smoke and fog. Smog can become so thick it actually reduces visibility (how far you can see) and can cause many kinds of respiratory problems. It has also been known to produce eye irritation and can damage many types of plants. In 1952, the smog in London was so thick it is believed to have caused about 4,000 deaths.

Although factories and airplanes are major causes of air pollution, individual people are a part of the problem as well. Each person who drives a vehicle to work or school each day contributes to the dangerous gases in the air. Widespread use of aerosol cans (spray cans using fluorocarbons) releases chemicals that reduce the ozone layer, a gas which helps protect the earth's atmosphere. Burning leaves or rubbish puts many pollutants into the air and contribute to the problem.

Some things are being done to help reduce the amount of smog. Special devices have been added to motor vehicles to reduce the amount of dangerous gases they produce. Laws have been passed to force industries to reduce the amount of pollutants they produce. Gasoline companies have stopped adding lead to their product, reducing the pollution it causes. Some cities have banned burning leaves and rubbish at any time. Other cities do not allow fires in stoves or fireplaces except on days when the wind is strong enough to carry the smoke away from the city. Aerosol cans have been replaced with pump sprays to reduce the use of fluorocarbons. Many individuals have formed car pools where groups of people ride to work or school together rather than each person taking his own vehicle.

The cost of cleaning up the air after it has been polluted is very high. Some methods of cleaning the air actually produce other forms of pollution that must be dealt with. Air pollution is certainly not an easy problem to solve! Although we have a long way to go before our air is clean again, many people are constantly working on new solutions to this big problem.

©1995 Kelley Wingate Publications   33   KW 1018

---

1. What is the main idea of this story?
   A. Many people in London died because of smog.
   B. Air pollution, and smog in particular, has created many health problems.
   C. Air is necessary to all living things.

2. What are some of the causes of pollution?
   power and heat generators; burning solid wastes; industries; transportation

3. What is smog?
   a combination of dirt and clouds

4. What are some problems caused by smog?
   it reduces visibility, can cause eye irritation and respiratory problems

5. What word means "ability to see at a distance"?
   A. smog
   B. visibility
   C. pollutant

6. Name three things that contribute to smog:
   driving vehicles to work or school; use of aerosol cans; burning leaves or rubbish

7. What is an "aerosol can"?
   a spray can that uses fluorocarbons

8. What is being done to reduce smog produced by vehicles?
   car-pools, emission control

9. How can individuals help reduce the amount of air pollution?
   car-pools, don't burn trash or leaves

10. Why is it so difficult to clean polluted air?
    cost is high and some methods of cleaning the air create other forms of pollution

THINK AHEAD: What can you do to help fight air pollution?

©1995 Kelley Wingate Publications   34   KW 1018

Answer Key

Name _____ Skill: comprehension

Acid Rain

Acid rain is a type of pollution that is creating many problems for the air, land, and water. Acid rain is formed when water vapor in the air condenses on sulfur and nitrogen dioxides. This acid filled water may sit over the land as a fog or it can fall as rain, snow, or hail. Acid rain has destroyed lakes containing plant and animal life, caused damage to forests and crops, and contaminated drinking water. Winds often carry these clouds great distances before the acid rain finally falls. The damaging affects of acid rain have been found in Europe, North America, and Africa.

Sulfur in the air comes mainly from the burning of oil or coal. Some factories that use these fuels are required to install expensive air cleaners called scrubbers in their smokestacks to reduce the amount of sulfur they release into the air. Other factories have begun to use coal with a lower sulfur content. Nitrogen oxides are generally produced from automobile engines. More people than ever own one or two cars so the problem has grown considerably in the past few years. Car manufacturers are now required to use devices that help reduce the amount of this dangerous gas.

1. **What is the main idea of this story?**
   A. Cars contribute to the formation of acid rain.
   B. Acid rain can be found in many parts of the world.
   C. Acid rain pollutes air, land, and water. *(C circled)*

2. **What is acid rain?**
   water vapor condensed on sulfur and nitrogen dioxides

3. **What are the damaging effects of acid rain?**
   acid rain ruins forests and crops and contaminates drinking water

4. **What are "scrubbers"?**
   A. devices that remove sulfur from the air *(A circled)*
   B. devices put on cars to remove nitrogen oxides
   C. contaminated drinking water

5. **What is the biggest producer of nitrogen oxide?**
   automobile engines

THINK AHEAD: Find out more about acid rain. What can be done to control this problem?

©1995 Kelley Wingate Publications   35   KW 1018

Name _____ Skill: comprehension

Recycling

In the past, materials used as containers or wraps were considered waste. They were burned, buried, or dumped into the ocean when they were no longer useful. Today people are more concerned with how our trash is being disposed of, or gotten rid of. We realize that trash cannot be burned because it releases harmful gases into the air. It cannot be buried because much of it never decomposes, or turns back into natural elements. (Plastic, for example, will remain in the same form for thousands of years!) Buried trash can also create chemicals that contaminate underground water supplies. Dumping trash into the ocean may seem like a quick solution, but we all know that this practice cannot continue or we will ruin the oceans, too.

Recycling is a very practical way of handling our trash. Some metals, paper, glass, and plastic can be recycled, or processed and used again. For example, a glass or plastic beverage container that is discarded will never decompose or melt down, but that is only half of the problem. A new bottle must be made to replace the one that was discarded. Materials that produce glass or plastic must be purchased and processed to produce the new bottle. If the bottle is recycled rather than discarded, it does not create waste or cost a lot to prepare for reuse.

Recycling products is a good control for pollution, but it is not without problems of its own. One problem is the separation of types of trash. Metal, paper, glass, and plastic cannot all be treated the same way if it is to be reused. Recycling programs in cities require people to separate their trash in groups of paper, glass, metal, plastic, and garbage (food waste). This process helps the recyclers in the sorting process, but separating trash is not as easy as it appears. People are not happy about having to set out five cans instead of the usual one garbage can.

New methods for separating the materials have been developed. Now people only need to separate the garbage from the trash. The garbage is hauled away and disposed of. Trash is taken to a processing plant where the lighter material (paper) is taken out. The paper is either burned to produce power or shredded and reformed as cardboard, paper bags, newsprint, and other paper products. The rest of the trash is put on a conveyor belt and sent down a line. The belt passes by electromagnet and other devices that separate the trash into groups of metal, plastic, and glass. The metals are sold as scrap to be melted down and reused. Plastics may be melted and reused or shredded for use as fiberfill. Glass is separated by color then melted and reused.

The energy used to reprocess waste materials is usually much less than it takes to make the same product from all new materials. Recycling, however, can end up costing more than new production because it involves collection, transportation, and separation of the used materials. Another problem is that melting waste products

©1995 Kelley Wingate Publications   36   KW 1018

---

requires very high temperatures, and waste gases are often a result. Solving the problem of one type of pollution can actually create pollution in another form!

Recycling trash is helpful, even though it is not perfect. Do not give up hope, however, because scientists and researchers are continuing to look for better solutions and techniques to improve the recycling process.

1. **What is the main idea of this story?**
   A. Recycling is one way of decreasing pollution, but it does have some problems of its own. *(A circled)*
   B. People do not like to separate their trash.
   C. Recycling is not a good idea.

2. **Why shouldn't trash be burned or buried?**
   burning trash releases harmful chemicals into the air; buried trash does not break down

3. **What does the word "recycle" mean?**
   A. separating into piles of like materials
   B. able to break down into natural elements
   C. reprocessed and used again *(C circled)*

4. **What was an early problem with recycling methods?**
   People did not like to separate their trash

5. **Name three products that can be made from recycled paper:**
   cardboard, paper bags, newsprint

6. **Name two problems with recycling:**
   It costs more than using new materials; it produces some pollution

THINK AHEAD: What types of trash does your community recycle? Plan a trip to visit a recycling plant.

©1995 Kelley Wingate Publications   37   KW 1018

Name _____ Skill: comprehension

Pollution Controls

People are interested in protecting the environment from the effects of pollution. We all know that any damage to the environment will eventually be harmful to human life as well. Since it is humans who create most of the pollution, it is humans who must find a way to deal with it.

There are four ways to manage pollution that are currently being used. The first method is to stop pollution producers during periods of high air pollution. When the level of air pollution is higher than normal, some factories are forced to close until conditions improve. Some cities outlaw burning of any materials, even logs in a fireplace, when air pollution is heavy. By stopping major producers of pollution when levels are high, we give the environment a chance to lessen the problem on its own.

The second method of pollution control is to lessen the concentration of emissions, or waste given off. Some cities require workers to car pool to their jobs, reducing the number of vehicles giving off exhaust. Factories are required to build tall smokestacks so that the gases are released further away from the ground. This gives the wind a chance to spread the gases around, creating lower concentration in any one area. This method helps control smog in manufacturing areas, but by spreading the gas further it exposes even more people to the pollution. Taller smokestacks are also cited as a reason for the increase in acid rain.

Thirdly, some pollutants can be removed from waste products before they are released into the air or water. This method is called emissions reductions (reducing the amount of waste released). This method cuts back on the pollutants that can be released into the environment, but it also creates a new problem. When the pollutant has been removed from the waste it must be stored somewhere. It is usually put in air-tight containers then buried or stored in waste dumps. Scientists do not know what to do with this waste product, so it continues to build up. Recent laws concerning these waste products have prompted research for ways to treat the waste and make it harmless.

The fourth method of pollution control is to change the manufacturing process so that it produces less pollution from the start. Many new industries are finding ways to build factories that are more "environmentally friendly", creating much less waste products. This method of pollution control has proven to be more effective and less costly than the other three methods.

Controlling pollution is a complex and difficult problem. The very products that make life easier are creating dangerous conditions for the environment. Scientists and researchers know we cannot stop driving cars or manufacturing products. That is not a realistic solution. They are working on ways that will bring a balance back between the needs of man and the needs of the environment. If we keep trying new ideas and looking for better methods the problem of pollution may someday be no problem at all!

©1995 Kelley Wingate Publications   38   KW 1018

Answer Key

Name _____ Skill: comprehension

---

1. **What is the main idea of this story?**
   A. Taller smokestacks spread pollution even farther.
   B. Some dangerous waste products are stored in barrels and buried.
   C. People are working to control the levels of pollution. *(C circled)*

2. **Why are people interested in protecting the environment from pollution?**
   because any damage to the environment will eventually be harmful to humans

3. **In your own words, restate the four methods of pollution control:**
   Control the amount of pollution at a given time
   Make less pollution - use products that produce less waste
   Remove pollutants and store them
   change the way we make things...

4. **Why is it useful for a factory to build a tall smoke stack?**
   so that gasses are released further away from the ground

5. **What is a disadvantage of taller smoke stacks?**
   they cause an increase in acid rain

6. **What is a problem with emissions reduction?**
   the removed pollutant must be stored somewhere. and it continues to build up...

7. **Car pools are an example of which method of pollution control?**
   emissions control

8. **What does the word "emission" mean?**
   A. changing the manufacturing process
   B. to give off *(B circled)*
   C. reducing waste products

9. **Which pollution control method is believed to be most efficient?**
   changing the way we manufacture things

THINK AHEAD: Does your community have any "environmentally friendly" factories?

Endangered Animals

The dinosaurs that once roamed the earth have all disappeared. Everyone is aware that they are extinct now, but we are fascinated with what they must have been like. We cannot observe them to find out about their habits, nor can we know for certain what they looked like. All that we know about dinosaurs comes from guesses and theories we develop as their remains are found.

Dinosaurs are not the only animals that have become extinct. Once, North America was full of animals called mammoths. They looked a lot like the modern day elephant, but they were covered with long hair. Hunters found mammoths to be a rich source of food, skins for clothing, and bones for tools. There were so many mammoths that people did not worry about wasting the meat or skin. The mammoths could not reproduce quickly enough to replace the numbers that were killed by hunters. It did not take long to wipe out the entire species. Today we have a pretty good idea of what the mammoth looked like because ancient cave artists left us a few drawings of these beasts.

During the past few hundred years man has hunted many animals to extinction. The moas (large flightless birds) of New Zealand were easy to kill and tasted pretty good. It took only 200 years to make the moas extinct. Dodo birds were found in abundance on the Maritius Islands in the Indian Ocean. It was a strange looking bird with a large head and short legs. They could not move quickly and were unable to fly. Dodo birds were so easy to catch that it only took 70 years for them to become extinct. The Stellar's sea cow, related to the manatee, took only 27 years to become extinct!

Food was not the only reason animals have been hunted into extinction or near extinction. The Carolina parakeet had beautiful feathers that were popular fashion trends for hats. That bird became extinct because people thought it was pretty. Beavers were hunted for many years because their fur was used to make coats and hats. By 1800 the beaver population had dropped drastically and they were much more difficult to find. Fortunately trends changed about then, and beaver was no longer desirable. The beavers were saved, not because they were nearing extinction but, rather, because their fur was not in fashion!

Many other animals have become endangered, or close to extinction. In the 1920's, thousands of elephants were killed for their ivory tusks. The ivory was fashioned into piano keys and billiard balls. The bald eagle was considered quite a trophy to stuff and hang on walls. It was hunted until there were very few left. Whales, sea turtles, and panda bears are a few examples of animals on the endangered species list.

Animals, like all our other natural resources, are not limitless. When one species becomes extinct, it is not just that animal that is affected. Other animals that

---

depended on that species for their own survival are affected, too. The entire ecological system is changed because of the disappearance of one species. The Endangered Species Act of 1973 is a law created to protect animals in danger of becoming extinct. The Act makes it a crime for anyone to sell or transport endangered animals or products made from endangered animals. The law also sets aside certain lands that are natural habitats (living areas) of these animals. By protecting these animals, we can prevent the needless extinction of any more of our wildlife. Our descendants in the future will not need to rely on books and pictures to tell them what elephants and whales looked like. They will be able to see the animals for themselves.

1. **What is the main idea of this story?**
   A. Dodo birds are extinct.
   B. It is important to prevent animals from becoming extinct. *(B circled)*
   C. The Endangered Species Act protects endangered animals.

2. **What was the cause for the extinction of many animals?**
   humans hunted them

3. **Name four animals that are now extinct:**
   dodo, moa, Stellar's sea cow, Carolina parakeet

4. **What does the word "habitat" mean?**
   A. place where a plant or animal naturally lives *(A circled)*
   B. near extinction
   C. a law protecting animals

5. **Name three animals that are on the endangered species list:**
   elephants, bald eagle, panda bear, whale, sea turtle

6. **Why is it important to save animals from extinction?**
   any extinction affects all other animal life.

THINK AHEAD: What areas near your community are protected as a habitat for endangered species?

Name _____ Skill: comprehension

National Parks

National parks are huge areas of land set aside to preserve the natural flora (plants) and fauna (animals). These parks are protected by law so that no one can use them for profit. People who go to national parks are considered to be visitors, and they are not allowed to hurt the animals or plants in any way. These parks are beautiful examples of nature at its best and are of great scientific, educational, and recreational value.

In the 1800's less than ten national parks existed in Canada, the United States, and Australia. As the world became aware of the dangers of pollution and extinction, many more parks were created to ensure that some of nature would remain in its original state. Since 1990, more than 100 countries have established national parks or reserves and there are now more than 2,000 such parks around the world!

Canada's first national park was established in 1885. Banff National Park in Alberta sits in the Rocky Mountains near the British Colombian border. It is known for its beautiful mountains, its glaciers, Lake Louise, and variety of wildlife. The United States established its first national park, Yellowstone, in 1872. It covers a large area that includes parts of Idaho, Montana, and Wyoming. Yellowstone is best known for having numerous geysers and hot springs, and for its breathtaking scenery. Australia established its first park in 1879.

The idea of national parks caught on and many were established during the late 1800's and early 1900's. New Zealand, South Africa, Sweden, Russia, France, and Switzerland were among the first countries to recognize the value of such reserves and quickly established their own. The world's highest mountains, largest waterfalls, and other important natural features on nearly every continent are now protected as national parks. Governments are eager to set aside as many parks as possible before civilization takes over and changes them forever.

National parks have run into several problems in protecting their natural environment, however. When native animals are given complete protection, as they are in national parks, they can reproduce rapidly and soon become a problem. For example, the Yellowstone elk and the African elephant have become so large in number they are endangering the survival of some plants and other smaller animals in the park! Another problem is the large number of visitors to the parks each year. So many tourists are attracted to the parks that control over misuse is difficult to enforce. The huge size of some parks makes them easy targets for poachers (illegal hunters).

Even with the problems that face them, national parks are wonderful areas that can make people appreciate nature and learn more about the world we live in. They are there for us to visit and enjoy. They will be there for future generations to visit and learn from as well!

Page 43

1. What is the main idea of this story?
   A. National parks can be found all over the world.
   (B) National parks are places set aside to preserve nature.
   C. Many plants and animals are safe in national parks.

2. What are national parks?
   large areas of land set aside to preserve plants and animals

3. How many national parks existed in the 1880's?
   less than ten

4. What is Banff National Park known for?
   its beautiful mountains, its glaciers, Lake Louise and its variety of wildlife

5. What does the word "fauna" mean?
   A. plants
   (B) wildlife
   C. national parks

6. Name two problems that national parks must deal with:
   poachers, over population of animals, too many visitors

7. Where would you find Banff National Park?
   Alberta, Canada

8. What is Yellowstone National Park famous for?
   geysers, hot springs and scenery

9. What is a poacher?
   A. a fried egg
   B. an angry deer
   (C) an illegal hunter

THINK AHEAD: What national park is closest to where you live? What are its outstanding features?

Page 44

Name _____

Transportation

From ancient times to today, people have tried to find better ways to transport themselves and their things from one place to another. The first major improvement of land transportation was when man began to domesticate, or tame, animals. Horses and mules were perfect for carrying a tired person or a load of items too heavy for one person to handle. The invention of the wheel was probably the second and most important step in transportation. The wheel allowed people to roll wagons and carts easily. When animals were attached to the cart, whole loads of heavy items could be moved at one time. Of course, the paths made for walking of animals was not wide enough for carts, so wider paths called roads were made. These wonderful inventions allowed people to travel at the quick pace of about six miles per hour. Carts, animals, and roads sure beat walking! Land transportation did not change much over the next three or four thousand years. There were some improvements like the horse collar and carriage springs, but the combination of animals and carts could not be outdone until the invention of trains during the 17th century. The first trains were horse-drawn wagons with wooden wheels and rails, used mainly in mining.

Water transportation probably began around the same time as domestic animal transportation. Someone probably noticed that a log would float in the water and climbed on the first boat! Little is known about early boats, but at some time the log was hollowed out and shaped to make it more stable. Eventually pushing sticks and paddles were added to make the boat move more rapidly through the water. Larger ships controlled by many oars and propelled, or moved by sails, increased the ability to move about from one land to another. The invention of the rudder (a flat piece of wood or metal used to steer boats) and the compass gave water transportation a real boost. Now, even larger ships could be built and they dared to venture farther into the oceans in search of adventure.

The invention of the steam engine around 1698 was one of the largest improvements to transportation. By the late 1700's the steam engine propelled boats and trains, vastly improving the speed at which anyone could travel! Steam engines controlled transportation for about eighty years until the internal combustion engine (gasoline motor) was invented in 1860. By 1890, the first "horseless carriages" were introduced and in 1912 came the first motorized airplane. Transportation would never again be the same! The first rocket was launched in 1926, and by 1969 man had landed on the moon.

Today's road systems, railways, airplanes, and connected waterways provide the fast and fairly inexpensive transportation man has always looked for. The same cross-country trip that took a horse and wagon four months to complete can now be made by car in four days or by plane in four hours.

Page 45

1. What is the main idea of this story?
   (A) Faster and better transportation has always been important to people.
   B. Transportation did not really improve until the invention of the steam engine.
   C. Rockets are the fastest means of transportation ever invented.

2. What was the first major improvement in land transportation?
   domestic animals

3. What did the wheel allow people to do?
   it allowed people to roll wagons or carts easily

4. How long did animals and carts remain as the best means of land transportation?
   until the 17th century

5. What did the first trains consist of?
   they were horse-drawn wagons with wooden wheels and rails

6. What does the word "propel" mean?
   A. to tame
   (B) to move forward
   C. to steer or guide

7. Which two inventions allowed sailors to travel the oceans?
   the rudder and the compass

8. What does the word "rudder" mean?
   A. to move forward
   B. to steer or guide
   (C) a flat piece of wood or metal used to steer boats and ships

9. How did the invention of the steam engine change transportation?
   it was much faster, easier and could carry much larger loads

THINK AHEAD: What types of transportation have you used? What do you predict transportation will be like 100 years from now?

Page 46

Name _____   Skill: comprehension

Roads and Highways

Getting from one point to another is much easier if there is a path or road. Think about walking through the woods. Trying to get around trees and through bushes is a difficult task. It is much easier to get where you are going if a path or trail has been cleared for you. Early travelers had much the same problem. The first person to walk through an area had to clear the way, or create a route. When people began to use carts and wagons, these paths had to be widened so the wheels could fit. Motorized vehicles were wider still than carts and wagons, thus making the roads even wider.

There are many words that describe different types of land routes. Tracks were probably the first type of route. A track is a route that is not terribly well marked, but is evident. If you have ever followed an animal by watching for the footprints, you have been on a track. A track that is used often and is clearly evident is called a path. A trail is a path that has been well worn until the ground has been packed down. A road is a narrow route, usually wide enough for two cars, and is found in rural (country) areas. A street is much like a road, but is found in urban (city) areas. A highway has several lanes going in each direction and is divided by raised curbs or grassy areas. Highways that have limited access (not many ways to get on or off) are called expressways or freeways. If you must pay a toll, or fee, to drive on the expressway it is called a turnpike. Names used in other countries include motorway (Great Britain), autobahn (Germany), autostrada (Italy) and autoroute(France).

Dirt roads worked well with carts and wagons for a very long time, but they were often dusty and muddy. As motorized vehicles became popular, the need for better roads arose. Some cities solved the problem by paving the streets with bricks or small stones. This was a difficult and rather expensive job. Long stretches of road through rural areas were treated differently. The first attempts at paving were made by laying small trees or saplings next to each other across the road. As you can imagine, these roads were very bumpy and quickly became known as "corduroy roads". Corduroy roads were not very popular and were soon replaced with sawed boards called planks. These plank roads made vehicle travel much easier. They were smooth and removed the problems of dust, puddles, and ruts associated with dirt roads. In rural areas today there are paved roads that still go by the name "plank". In the early 19th century, France was the first country to begin paving their roads with asphalt. These roads were very popular because they were very smooth and were dust proof. It was soon discovered that when asphalt becomes wet it also becomes slippery. About 1929 the asphalt roads were given a top layer of rough material that prevented the road from becoming so slippery. Most roads and highways today are constructed of concrete poured over a wire mesh to make them stronger.

Answer Key

Today much of the world is crisscrossed with roads and highways that can take vehicles from the deserts of Egypt to the rainforests of Brazil. Travel is much easier than it was only 100 years ago. Just think what the next 100 years will bring!

1. **What is the main idea of this story?**
   A. Roads were first paved in 1929.
   B. Dirt roads were too dusty and bumpy for motorized vehicles.
   C. Roads have developed from dirt paths to multilane expressways.

2. **What is the difference between a road and a highway?**
   A road has two lanes; a highway has limited access, is divided and has two or more lanes.

3. **What is the difference between a corduroy and a plank road?**
   Corduroy roads were made by laying small trees next to each other; Plank roads were made by laying sawed boards called planks

4. **What does the word "urban" mean?**
   A. of the city
   B. of the country
   C. street

5. **Where would you find an "autoroute"?**
   A. France
   B. Canada
   C. in a forest

6. **Which country is credited with being the first to use asphalt as a road cover?**
   France used asphalt roads in the early 19th century

7. **What was the main problem with asphalt roads?**
   they were slippery when wet

8. **Why do motorized vehicles need smoother roads than wagons and carts do?**
   they travel much faster, so bumps affected them more than they affected carts

THINK AHEAD: Describe what you think the roads will be like 100 years from now.

Name _____ Skill: comprehension

World Highways

Roads allow us to go from place to place quickly and easily. Roads are connections from one place to another. They are used as an easy means to transport goods, carry messages, and visit other places. The importance of roads as connections between places was established many thousands of years ago.

As early as 3,000 B.C., road systems had been developed in Egypt and Mesopotamia. By 200 B.C., the Ch'in dynasty in China had built a road system that covered most of the country. The Incas of South America never discovered the wheel, and yet they had a well maintained road system that stretched about 2,300 miles! Early Romans recognized the importance of roads and established an excellent system that provided a connection for the entire empire.

Road systems continue to be an important link between towns, cities, and countries today. They provide easy access between places and have contributed greatly to international trade. Goods can be shipped quickly and inexpensively by highway. Today's highway systems are extensive and usually well maintained.

One of the longest highway systems in the world is the Pan American Highway. Construction on this highway began in 1923, and parts of it are still not completed. The Pan American Highway is about 26,000 miles long and connects Canada, the United States, Mexico, Central America, and South America. The highway crosses desert, dense tropical jungle, and high mountain passes. It has been mostly completed except for two sections - the isthmus of Panama and the Darien Gap. The Pan American Highway ends in Santiago in central Chile.

Many countries have excellent highway systems. Germany has constructed a highway system that extends about 2,500 miles between Bonn and Cologne. The Autobahn was begun under Hitler, but grew considerably after World War II. The motorway was built with fast travel in mind so there are no speed limits. Canada has several important national and international roadways. The Trans-Canada Highway was begun in 1962 and completed in 1965. Covering 4,860 miles, it is the longest national highway in the world. Another Canadian highway, the Alaska Highway, was built to connect Alaska with the continental United States. This roadway extends 2,452 miles from Dawson Creek, British Columbia to Fairbanks, Alaska. It was first used a military supply route, but was opened to the public in 1947.

Although speed is an important factor of highways, it is not the only consideration. Driving along stretches of road can become very boring and cause the driver to become sleepy. Modern highway planners try to select areas that are suitable to construction and provide scenic areas that help to keep drivers alert. Another problem for planners is how to connect road systems without destroying part of the city itself. Raised roadways, tunnels, and overpasses are designed so new roads can go over or under the land with little disruption to what is already there.

---

1. **What is the main idea of this story?**
   A. Road systems have been an important connection for people.
   B. The Trans-Canada Highway is the longest road in the world.
   C. Roads are designed for both speed and safety.

2. **Where were the earliest road systems built?**
   Egypt and Mesopotamia

3. **What is the importance of road systems?**
   they link places together

4. **What is the longest national highway in the world?**
   the Trans-Canada highway

5. **Which highway system links all of the American countries?**
   the Pan-American Highway

6. **Name three large highway systems:**
   Auto bahn, ALaskan Highway, the Trans-Canada Highway...

7. **What two area does the Alaska Highway connect? What was it first used for?**
   Alaska and the United States

8. **How do highway planners avoid tearing down everything in order to build new roads?**
   planners use raised roads, tunnels and overpasses

9. **What kinds of areas do highway planners try to select for building new highways? Why?**
   scenic areas that are suitable for construction
   to help keep drivers alert

THINK AHEAD: What international highway system is closest to where you live?

Name _____ Skill: comprehension

Bridges

A problem that faced all road builders was how to span natural obstacles, or things that were in the way. Roads were built across all kinds of terrain from mountains to ravines to rivers. One structure that helped cross ravines and rivers was the bridge. The earliest bridges were probably tree trunks or flat stones thrown across a stream. This method of providing a span is known as beam bridges. As better means of transportation developed, so did the need for better bridges.

Early bridges were also built by suspension, or hanging. These bridges consisted of twisted bamboo or vines tied to tree trunks on either side of the obstacle to be crossed. Thick sticks or boards were tied to the vines so they could be crossed easily. Bridges of this type can still be found in parts of Africa and Asia.

Some of the finest bridges of early times were constructed by the Romans. They gave us many of the building techniques that are still in use today. The Romans discovered a type of cement that could be used to build foundations that extended into the water. Roman bridges were semicircular arches that were made of stone or brick. This method of construction is known as arch bridges. The Roman bridges were impressive, some standing as tall as 98 feet high. These bridges were very well built and many are still standing today.

The 14th through the 16th centuries was another great era for building bridges. Advancements were made in methods of anchoring, or holding the bridge in place, across fairly long distances. Arches needed to be large enough so that ships might pass under them. Piles were driven into the water to provide a support for the arch ends where they came down into the water. Bridges became like works of art to be enjoyed as well as useful. Several wide bridges built during this time were wide enough to allow room for small shops along the sides!

The use of iron during the 18th and 19th centuries made bridge designing easier than ever. Iron could be shaped, bolted together, and was very strong. In 1791 the first all iron bridge was built over the River Severn in England. The use of iron also allowed suspension bridges to hold a great deal of weight. Strong metal cables were used to support two lanes of roadway over distances of up to 600 feet. The finest example of the early suspension bridge is the Brooklyn Bridge built in the late 1800's. Four main cables support six lanes of traffic and a wide footbridge that spans almost 1,600 feet! The Brooklyn Bridge is still an important connection between Brooklyn and Manhattan.

Many modern bridges must be movable to allow large ships to pass. Vehicles are stopped while sections of the bridge are moved for water traffic. Bascule bridges swing upward at one end or in the middle to create an opening. Lift bridges have a section that remains horizontal while weights at each end are lowered, lifting the bridge

---

section high above the water. Other bridges rest on a pivot or pin. A section of the bridge actually turns sideways, allowing ships to pass beside it. The development of stronger supports allows new bridges to be built at such heights that even the tallest ships can easily pass under without interrupting the traffic.

1. What is the main idea of this story?
A. Bridges have movable sections to allow ships to pass.
B. Early bridges were made of stones or tree trunks.
(C) Bridges were built, allowing roads to be built over natural obstacles.

2. What early people built the finest bridges for their time?
The Romans

3. Another word for "suspension" is:
A. moving
B. driving
(C) hanging

3. How did the discovery of iron help build better bridges?
the use of iron allowed for better design, strength, and suspension bridges

4. What does the word "obstacle" mean?
A. a bridge that swings sideways
(B) something that is in the way
C. having strong anchors

5. What three things were special about bridges built in the 14th, 15th, and 16th centuries?
① well anchored; ② boats could pass under them ③ piles were driven as supports ...

6. Why was there a need for movable bridges?
boats were getting larger and could not fit under bridges, so the bridge would be moved

7. What is a Bascule bridge?
a bridge that swings upward at one end or in the middle to create an opening

THINK AHEAD: Find the name of the longest single suspension bridge in the world.

©1995 Kelley Wingate Publications   51   KW 1018

Name _____   Skill: comprehension

London Bridge
Almost every small child has heard the nursery rhyme about London Bridge and how it is falling down. The rhyme was based on the actual history of this old bridge. London Bridge is the name of three bridges constructed in the same spot over the Thames River in England.

The first structure, called Old London Bridge, was built during the 1100's. It was among the last of the timber (wooden) bridges to be built over the Thames. Old London Bridge has 19 arches that rested on wide piers built in the river. The bridge was very wide and many wooden shops and homes were built along the sides. The bridge was damaged many times when the wooden buildings caught fire. This occurred so many times it seemed as though the bridge was constantly being rebuilt. The bridge "fell down" so many times it became the subject of the nursery rhyme. The shops and houses were finally removed from the bridge in 1763.

Old London Bridge was replaced by a five arched masonry (stone or brick) structure in 1831. The masonry bridge was replaced in 1967 with a six lane concrete bridge. The stone bridge was sold, carefully taken apart, and reconstructed in Lake Havasu City, Arizona where it stands today.

1. What is the main idea of this story?
(A) London Bridge was the name of three different bridges built in the same spot.
B. London Bridge is the subject of a nursery rhyme.
C. London Bridge burned many times.

2. What was the biggest problem with Old London Bridge?
it was made of wood and often burned

3. What happened to the second London Bridge?
it was removed and rebuilt in Arizona

4. When was the third London Bridge constructed?
1967

5. How many arches did Old London Bridge have? How many did the second London Bridge have?
Old London Bridge - 19 arches
Second Bridge - 5 arches

THINK AHEAD: What problems do you think might be caused by putting shops and homes on bridges today?

©1995 Kelley Wingate Publications   52   KW 1018

Name _____   Skill: comprehension

Tunnels
Road builders had a special challenge when they came to mountain areas. The roads had to climb gradually, turning and twisting as they went up or down the steep sides. Miles of road had to be laid just to cross over a few miles. During the 1800's the increasing use of railroads caused builders to consider new ideas about crossing the mountains. The most direct route was, of course, a tunnel straight through the mountain.

Digging a tunnel was not a new idea. Early cave dwellers tunneled to make a natural cave bigger. Babylonians dug tunnels for irrigation of crops. Egyptians created tunnels for tombs and temple rooms in the pyramids. The ancient Greeks used tunnels to bring water to their villages. One tunnel, built on the island of Samos in the 6th century B.C., was about 3,000 feet long. The Romans also dug a tunnel to connect the city of Pozzuoli with Naples. This tunnel, cut through rock, was 4,800 feet long and 25 feet wide.

During the 1800's tunneling techniques improved with the use of drills and dynamite. These methods were used to dig the 8.5 mile long Mont Cenis Tunnel through the mountains between Italy and France in 1857-71. At about the same time other major tunnels were being built elsewhere. The Hoosac Tunnel (1872-82) was built through the Berkshires in the United States. The First Simplon Tunnel (1898-1906) connected Italy and Switzerland with twelve miles of tunnel. The First Simplon held the record of the longest transportation tunnel in the world for many years.

As rock tunneling developed, so did the idea of subaqueous (under water) tunneling. Subaqueous tunnels are holes dug through the ground below a river or other body of water. A French engineer named Marc Brunel developed a shield for tunneling under rivers. The shield was a large rectangular box where 36 diggers could work at the same time. The first underwater tunnel was built in 1825-43 through the Thames River in England. In 1906-10 a new kind of tunnel connecting Detroit, Michigan and Windsor, Ontario was built in the Detroit River. This tunnel went through the water rather than under it. The tunnel was built in sections and sealed closed. The sections were sunk to the bottom of the river and connected together by divers. The tunnel was then covered for protection. Japanese railroad tunnels were the first tunnels built under the ocean (1936-44). The Seikan Tunnel connects the Japanese islands of Honshu and Hokkaido and is 33 miles long.

Subways are common tunnels found in most major cities. These tunnels are formed by digging deep trenches in the ground, building the tunnels, then covering the tunnel over with dirt. Subways provide an efficient method of transportation without using valuable ground space, as roads do.

©1995 Kelley Wingate Publications   53   KW 1018

---

1. What is the main idea of this story?
A. The use of railroads created the need for tunnels.
B. Tunnels were invented by cave dwellers.
(C) Tunnels provide direct transportation routes without using valuable above ground space.

2. How must roads be constucted in mountain areas?
by digging a tunnel straight through the mountain

3. For what purpose did ancient Greeks build tunnels?
to bring water to their villages

4. What did the 4,800 foot long Roman tunnel connect?
the cities of Pozzuoli and Naples

5. What two techniques improved tunneling during the 1800's?
drills and dynamite

6. What does the word "subaqueous" mean?
A. a tunnel for subways
(B) under water
C. a Roman tunnel that carried water to villages

7. Who invented the shield for tunneling under water?
Marc Brunel

8. How is the Detroit/Windsor tunnel different from most under water tunnels?
it lays on the bottom of the river

7. What were the first tunnels built under the ocean?
Japanese railroad tunnels

THINK AHEAD: What is the longest subaqueous tunnel in the world today?

©1995 Kelley Wingate Publications   54   KW 1018

Answer Key

Name _____   Skill: comprehension

The Chunnel

The English Channel is a section of the Atlantic Ocean that separates England and France. It is 21 to 150 miles wide and 565 feet deep. The strong waves in the channel have often made passage across it dangerous. In the 1880's, advances in tunneling convinced the British to try to dig a tunnel under the channel. Efforts were abandoned at that time because the British were afraid that such a tunnel could be used in an invasion attempt. The idea came up again around 1970, but was once more put aside, this time in favor of developing the supersonic Concorde jet.

Until recently the main transportation across the English Channel has been ferry boats and hovercraft. In 1986, France and Great Britain decided to join in the construction of the tunnel under the channel. The popular name for this project has become the "Chunnel". The plan was to dig a railway tunnel with each country starting on their own side of the channel. Work began in 1988. On December 1, 1990 the digging crews on both sides finally met in the middle of the channel. The Chunnel was opened for use in 1994.

1. What is the main idea of this story?
   A. The Chunnel is a railway tunnel.
   B. The French and English dug a tunnel.
   C. The Chunnel is a railway tunnel connecting France and England.

2. How wide is the English Channel?
   21 to 150 miles wide

3. When did the British first decide to dig a tunnel under the channel?
   In the 1880's

4. What was the main means of transportation across the channel before the Chunnel was opened?
   ferry boats and hovercraft

5. When did the Chunnel open for public use?
   1994

THINK AHEAD: Find out more about the Chunnel. How long is it? How long does it take to cross the channel using the chunnel?

Name _____   Skill: comprehension

Canals

Canals are man-made channels constructed for three main purposes. First, some canals are built for drainage of excess water. For example, the city of New Orleans in Louisiana has a canal drainage system. After a heavy rain the excess water is directed to the canals through drainpipes. The canals move the water toward pumping stations located on the Mississippi River and Lake Pontchartrain. The pumping stations pump the excess water over the levees (protective walls) and dump it into the river and lake. The canal systems help keep the city from flooding.

A second use for canals is to help ships bypass hazards on rivers. Canals of this type are most often used when the water level suddenly changes, usually near falls or rapids. Devices called locks are used in situations like these. Locks are like elevators for ships. A series of heavy doors are used to create a temporary dam across the water. To illustrate the point, imagine a ship on the higher side of a small waterfall. It certainly cannot go over the falls to continue its journey, so it is guided into a canal that goes around the falls. In the middle of the canal stands a heavy metal door, the first door on the lock. The door opens, the ship enters, and the door closes behind it. At the other end of the lock is another heavy metal door which is closed. The water level in the lock is the same as the high side of the falls. As the ship sits in the lock, water is slowly released and the water level begins to drop. When the water level is equal to the level below the falls the second door opens and the ship leaves. When a ship needs to go from the lower level to the higher level, water is pumped into the lock until it matches the higher water level.

For thousands of years water has been an important and inexpensive means for transporting large cargoes or cargoes that do not require fast delivery. Cargo such as coal, timber, grain, and chemicals can be loaded onto ships in large quantities and transported across oceans to the countries where they are needed. Getting the cargo inland where it would be used presented some problems, however. Some large ports were on inland waterways and there was no reasonable way to reach them. Canals have helped to solve this problem.

A third use for canals is to link bodies of water together. These are called ship or sea canals and can be found in many places around the world. Famous examples are the Suez Canal joining Africa and Asia, the Panama Canal joining the Atlantic and Pacific Oceans, the Erie Canal connecting Lake Erie and the Hudson River, and the Welland Canal linking Lake Ontario and Lake Erie. These canals provide an important link between manufacturing areas and the seaports where raw materials are imported.

---

1. What is the main idea of this story?
   A. Canals link bodies of water to one another.
   B. Canals are used in three important ways.
   C. Canals are used to transport goods by water.

2. Name the three uses for canals described in this passage:
   to transport water
   to by pass hazards
   to link bodies of water

3. What are locks used for?
   to help ships over falls, rapids, or changes in water level

4. What does the word "levee" mean?
   A. drainage canal
   B. to transport by canal
   C. a protective wall to keep water out

5. What is the reason for connecting large bodies of water?
   to link manufacturing areas with seaports

6. Name three major canals:
   Suez, Panama, Erie

THINK AHEAD: Which canal is the longest in the world? Where is it located?

Name _____   Skill: comprehension

Suez and Panama Canals

Two of the most important canals in the world are the Suez and the Panama. The Suez Canal is located between Asia and Africa, helping to link the Mediterranean Sea, the Red Sea, and the Indian Ocean. Before this canal was opened in 1869, European and East African ships that wanted to go to the Far East had to sail all the way around Africa. The Suez Canal provided a shorter route, cutting the distance in half in some cases. By 1888 the canal was recognized as an important world route and all ships of all nations were guaranteed freedom to use it.

The Suez Canal is owned and operated by Egypt. It begins at Port Said and ends at Port Taufiq, cutting across marshes and desert areas. The canal is 105 miles long and takes about 15 hours to go from one end to the other. During the 1960's about 15 percent of all world trade came through the Suez Canal. A great deal of that trade was petroleum (raw oil) that came from the Persian Gulf. As the world became more dependent on oil, ships called supertankers were created to transport larger quantities. The Suez Canal was too narrow for these big ships, and use of the canal dropped. Between 1975 and 1980 only about 4 percent of the world trade passed through the Suez Canal. Since that time the canal has been widened and deepened to accommodate these larger ships.

The Panama Canal crosses the Isthmus of Panama to connect the Atlantic and Pacific Oceans. Early sailors had to go around South America to get from one ocean to the other. The idea of building a canal across Panama originated during the early 16th century, but the technology to do it had not yet been developed. In 1881 a French company bought the rights to the canal and began to dig. The land was difficult to clear and many workers suffered from malaria or yellow fever. Work on the canal came to a halt in 1887. In 1904 the United States bought the rights to build the canal. By 1904 they had begun construction and completed the project in 1914. The total cost of the canal was about 3.5 million dollars.

Because of the difficult land and the great distance the canal covered, it was hailed as the greatest engineering creation of the modern age. The canal is 7,000 miles long, 300 feet wide, and at least 41 feet deep. Cristobal is the city that sits on the Atlantic side with Balboa on the Pacific. The canal has six sets of locks that raise and lower the ships to the proper level for each ocean. It takes about eight hours to cross from one ocean to the other.

The canal continued to be a great success for many years. During the 1970's and 80's, however, the development of wider ships created problems for passage through the canal. Work to widen the canal began in 1991, but is not yet completed.

Answer Key

Page 59

1. **What is the main idea of this story?**
   A. The Suez and Panama Canals are important world water routes. *(circled)*
   B. The Panama Canal is longer than the Suez Canal.
   C. The Suez Canal was built before the Panama Canal.

2. **How did European and East African ships reach the Far East before the Suez Canal was built?**
   They had to sail all the way around Africa.

3. **Why did use of the Suez Canal drop between 1975 and 1980?**
   The canal was too narrow for super-tankers to pass through.

4. **In what year did each of the canals open?**
   Suez - 1869   Panama - 1914

5. **What is the length of each canal?**
   Suez 105 miles
   Panama 7000 miles

6. **What does the word "petroleum" mean?**
   A. a water route across desert land
   B. raw oil *(circled)*
   C. malaria

7. **Who began work on the Panama Canal in 1881?**
   A French company

8. **Why did work on the Panama Canal stop in 1887?**
   The land was difficult to clear and many workers suffered from malaria or yellow fever.

9. **What was the final cost of building the Panama Canal?**
   3.5 million

10. **What bodies of water does each of the canals connect?**
    Suez - Connects Mediterranean to Red Sea and Indian Ocean — Panama - connects Pacific and Atlantic Ocean

THINK AHEAD: Look at a map of North and South America. Explain why early sailors felt Panama was a good place to dig a canal.

59   KW 1018

Page 60

Name _____   Skill: comprehension

Railroads

Railroads were first introduced in the 1500's and were used in England's mining operations. These first "trains" were wagons set on wooden rails and pulled by horses. During the 1700's they became more useful when they were outfitted with cast-iron wheels and rails, but they still were not very popular modes of transportation. The invention of the steam engine during the mid 1700's was just what the trains needed to become successful. The first public transportation railway was opened in 1825 in England. This 20 mile railroad opened the world's eyes to a new mode of transportation, the steam powered train.

It did not take long for people to realize that travel by train was superior to wagons, canals, and even steamboats. Trains were faster and more direct than water routes, cheaper and easier than wagon travel, and dependable throughout the year. During the 1800's, railroads began to pop up all over the world. France, Belgium, Germany, Italy, the Netherlands, and Russia all had railroads in operation by 1830. Canada opened its first rail service in 1836, and by 1880 had almost 7,000 miles of track. The Canadian Pacific Railway was completed across the Rockies to the Pacific by 1885. In 1860 the United States had over 30,000 miles of rail crossing the country.

Early passenger cars were similar to stagecoaches or wagons. Before long the cars were lengthened and could hold 40 to 50 people. Around 1860, sleeping cars were introduced so passengers could stretch out and relax on their journey. In the late 1860's, George Pullman designed dining and sleeping cars for railway lines. They were elaborate and comfortable, setting the standard of passenger cars for many years. By 1890 many coaches (passenger cars) were equipped with electric lights, heat, and covered passageways between cars.

Longer and heavier cars created a need for stronger locomotives, or engines. By the early 1900's the steam engine was being replaced with electric locomotives for high speed trains and diesel-electric locomotives for long distance travel. In 1964 the Japanese began to operate the now famous electric engine "bullet" train. It is capable of traveling at speeds up to 160 miles per hour. The trains have 16 cars that are permanently linked together and have four motors each. In 1981 The French completed a train which travels over steep inclines going as fast as 170 miles per hour.

The most recent train design does not have steel tracks or wheels. As a matter of fact it has no wheels at all! The Maglev (magnetic levitation train) glides over a magnetic field that raises it above the track. Other magnetic systems guide the train, make it stop, or add speed when needed. The Germans and the Japanese have been working to perfect this new train. Experimental models of the Maglev have traveled at speeds up to 300 miles per hour!

60   KW 1018

Page 61

1. **What is the main idea of this story?**
   A. Trains are cheaper and faster than wagons.
   B. Railroads have been an important means of transportation throughout the world. *(circled)*
   C. The steam engine helped the popularity of trains.

2. **Describe the very first railroad:**
   wagons on wooden tracks pulled by horses

3. **In what ways were trains better than other modes of transportation?**
   trains were faster, cheaper and easier than wagons and boats

4. **What does the word "coaches" mean in this passage?**
   A. teachers
   B. trains with wooden tracks
   C. passenger cars of a train *(circled)*

5. **How had trains been improved by 1890?**
   electric light, heat, and covered passageways between cars

6. **What change was made to locomotives in the early 1900's?**
   they were switched to electric engines

7. **Why did electric locomotives become necessary?**
   for long distance travel

8. **How fast does the Japanese "bullet" travel?**
   160 miles per hour

9. **What makes the Maglev travel so fast?**
   it glides over and is pulled by magnets

THINK AHEAD: How do you think the Maglev will affect the way people travel in the future?

61   KW 1018

Page 62

Name _____   Skill: comprehension

Above and Below Ground

In 1850, the common mode of local transportation was the horse and carriage. Major cities experienced the first traffic jams as the streets filled with carriages each day. It was apparent that cities needed to find an efficient way to move large quantities of people in shorter time periods. This was the birth of rapid transit systems (quick transport). Trains had become the most common means of transportation at this time, so it was only natural that cities looked to them as a solution.

In 1863, London became the first city to boast an underground railway system which quickly became known as the "tube". The subway had been born! Streets were removed while tunnels were dug below them. The walls and ceiling of the tunnel were constructed then covered with dirt. The roads were replaced directly over the tunnel. This is the most common way to build a subway and has been aptly named the "cut and cover" method. The subway worked well and soon other cities were building them as well.

New York City was also deeply congested with traffic and the idea of a subway interested them. However, Manhattan was built on granite, a very hard rock, and digging tunnels was not a wise idea at the time. Instead, New York looked up for the answer to their traffic problems. By 1868 New York had constructed elevated railways, commonly known as "els", that ran above the streets rather than under them. Els were railroad tracks that ran on a platform held above the streets by steel or concrete columns. Other cities, like Chicago, that had difficulty with tunneling also constructed elevated railways. The subway was far more popular in Europe, but only Hamburg and Liverpool built elevated systems.

These first rapid transit subways and els were powered by a steam engine locomotive, just as the regular ground trains were. They pulled between two and ten wooden passenger cars, or coaches. Each coach had several doors so the train could be quickly loaded and unloaded. The steam released from the locomotive created some operating problems, especially inside the subway tunnels. By 1890 the old steam engines were replaced by the cleaner and more efficient electric motors. A third track conducting electricity was placed next to the train tracks, supplying the train with electricity to move. Electricity is still used to power most subways today. Operators control the speed of the train by regulating the amount of electricity the motors receive.

By 1945, tunneling techniques had improved and New York began to build subways as well. The elevated trains were replaced by the subway in Manhattan, but remained in many suburbs of the city and are still in use today. Many portions of Chicago's el were also removed, but the "loop" in the middle of the city is still very busy.

62   KW 1018

Answer Key

Today, every major capital in the world has a subway system. Many are unique in the way they have made their subway safe or pleasant. Mexico City suspended their tunnels to absorb shock waves from earthquakes. Montreal uses rubber tires on their subway, making it the quietest one in the world. Hong Kong has the first fully air conditioned subway. These underground trains move thousands of people each day and have indeed lived up to their title of "rapid transit".

1. What is the main idea of this story?
   A. In 1850 cities experience their first traffic jams.
   B. More cities prefer subways to elevated trains.
   C. Elevated trains and subways are two forms of rapid transit systems.
2. Why was rapid transit needed as early as 1850?
   urban streets were crowded with horses and wagons
3. Which city had the first subway, and what year was it built?
   London built the first subway in 1863.
4. What does the word "granite" mean?
   A. a third track conducting electricity
   B. a type of rock
   C. a method of digging subway tunnels
5. What powered the first subways and elevated trains?
   steam engine locomotives
6. Describe the first coaches:
   wooden cars with several doors
7. Which two European cities built an elevated system?
   Hamburg and Liverpool
8. What is unique about Montreal's subway?
   It has rubber wheels for quieter rides

THINK AHEAD: How do you think the used of magnetically powered trains (like the Maglev) will affect subway transportation?

©1995 Kelley Wingate Publications   63   KW 1018

Name _____   Skill: cloze

Cloze is a reading exercise where some of the words are missing and you must put them back in. Read the story below. Every tenth word has been taken out and is listed below the passage. Fill in the blanks with the words you think will make sense.

a	far	go	had	had	I	I	It	looked	many	mile
morning	Saturday	The	the	the	the	when	worn			

Lost!

The cold wind was bitter so I pulled my coat even tighter around my neck. Thank goodness I had followed my mother's advice and *worn* mittens and a hat. Little did I know this *morning* I would end up lost in the woods during *a* snowstorm! The day had started out so nicely. Cindy *had* invited me to her house for lunch and, being *Saturday* with nothing to do, I immediately said I would *go*. The sun was shining and the snow covered trees *looked* so beautiful as I set out across the woods. *The* path was snowy, but packed down because Cindy and *I* had dragged our sleds over it so many times *the* past few days. Besides, it was only a half *mile* to Cindy's house and I had walked the trail *many* times I would have known the way even without *the* trail. When I got to her house, Cindy and *I* had hot chocolate and played in the back yard. *It* was early afternoon when I started for home, but *the* sky was dark and threatening to snow. The wind *had* picked up, too. I was barely into the woods *when* the blizzard hit, making it difficult to see very *far* ahead. The trail was quickly lost under the falling snow. Now I was lost and had no idea which way to go.

©1995 Kelley Wingate Publications   64   KW 1018

Name _____   Skill: cloze

Cloze is a reading exercise where some of the words are missing and you must put them back in. Read the story below. Every tenth word has been taken out and is listed below the passage. Fill in the blanks with the words you think will make sense.

a	a	best	each	front	her	if	made	nip	of
round	that	The	the	the	There	they	This		

Fish

The fish swam soothingly through the water in the tank. I had been watching them for almost an hour. *There* was something peaceful and calming about the fish that *made* me feel good. I was even beginning to feel *that* I knew each individual fish as if it were *a* friend! The orange and white fish stayed together all *the* time. It was funny to watch the one in *front* turn quickly while the other three followed. I thought *they* might bump into each other, but they never did. *The* two large yellow fish seemed to stay away from *each* other. If one came too near, the other would *nip* at its tail or fin. They reminded me of *a* couple having a quarrel. The fish I liked the *best* was the smallest one of all. She had a *round* shape with a white front and a black tail. *This* little fish was hiding among the rocks most of *the* time. Every few minutes she might join the others. As soon as any *of* the other fish came near she would return to *her* hiding spot. I could almost imagine that I was a fish swimming in there with them!

©1995 Kelley Wingate Publications   65   KW 1018

Name _____   Skill: cloze

Cloze is a reading exercise where some of the words are missing and you must put them back in. Read the story below. Every tenth word has been taken out and is listed below the passage. Fill in the blanks with the words you think will make sense.

book	had	he	he	Last	meant	planned	promised	really
relatives	study	test	they	was	worried			

The Test

Marty wiped the sweat from his face and looked at the clock. Class would begin in one minute and Marty was *worried*. Today Ms. Freble was giving the class a geography *test* and Marty was not at all prepared. He had *meant* to study but things kept getting in the way. *Last* Thursday he took his book and notes home and *planned* to look through them. Then Max came over and *they* played pool instead. Marty was not worried then because *he* still had three days left for studying. Friday night *was* the basketball game so, of course, he could not *study* then. Saturday Marty got as far as opening his *book* when Brian called. They went to the movie Marty *had* wanted to see and got home pretty late. Marty *promised* himself he would study the next day. Was it *really* his fault that his parents decided to go visit *relatives*? Marty knew he could not think about geography when *he* was busy talking to his cousin. Now here it was, Monday, and Marty had not even looked at his notes.

©1995 Kelley Wingate Publications   66   KW 1018

©1995 Kelley Wingate Publications   118   CD-3715

Answer Key

Name _____ Skill: cloze

Cloze is a reading exercise where some of the words are missing and you must put them back in. Read the story below. Every tenth word has been taken out and is listed below the passage. Fill in the blanks with the words you think will make sense.

an	and	animal	by	just	lumbered	perfect	quietly	silver	small
snuggled	sticks	The	the	their	through	two	up	watched	water
			were	where					

Univited Guest

R.J. and Michael dragged the heavy bag of supplies across the lawn and pushed it into the tent. That was the last of what they needed for **their** camp out in the backyard. The boys had erected **the** tent early in the morning. They set it out **by** the pond so they could barely see the house **through** the trees. The brothers had planned this event for **two** weeks so they were sure that everything would be **perfect** ! As the day turned into dusk, R.J. built a **small** fire and Michael took out the frankfurters and roasting **sticks** . Dinner was delicious. Soon it was dark and stars **were** shining from a million different spots in the sky. **The** moon was full and its bright light cast a **silver** glow on the tent. Frogs began their night croaking **and** crickets hummed in the grass. Suddenly Michael sat straight **up** and quietly pointed at the pond. R.J. looked to **where** Michael was pointing and saw the shadowy shape of **an** animal at the edge of the water. They heard **water** splash as the animal took a drink. Then it **lumbered** across the yard, straight for their tent. As the **animal** came nearer, the glow from the dying fire cast **just** enough light to see what it was. The boys **watched** as the huge skunk walked into their tent and **snuggled** down on a sleeping bag. The boys got up **quietly** and headed for the house. They knew that they could not have planned anything to avoid this situation!

©1995 Kelley Wingate Publications 67 KW 1018

Name _____ Skill: cloze

Cloze is a reading exercise where some of the words are missing and you must put them back in. Read the story below. Every eighth word has been taken out and is listed below the passage. Fill in the blanks with the words you think will make sense.

America	Arabian	called	countries	do	eating	fingers	is	meals	of
one	other	people	spoon	spoons	tables	their	times	use	

Eating Out

When you eat and how you eat depends on where you live. Meal times and utensils are a matter **of** custom, or what our culture has decided **is** best for the way we live. Many **countries** eat three meals a day. They are **called** breakfast, lunch, and dinner (or supper). Some **other** countries, like England and Norway, eat four **meals** a day. They have an afternoon "tea", **eating** dinner much later in the evening. Most **people** use utensils to eat formal meals. North **America** and most of Europe sit down at **tables** and eat with a knife, fork, and **spoon** . The eastern countries of Asia prefer to **use** chopsticks and bowls for their food. They **do** not use knives at the table because **their** food is prepared in small pieces. Many **Arabian** families in the Middle East eat from **one** large bowl, using either their fingers or **spoons** . Most places in the world use their **fingers** to eat certain foods or at special **times** . Can you imagine trying to eat a hamburger with a knife and fork?

©1995 Kelley Wingate Publications 68 KW 1018

Name _____ Skill: cloze

Cloze is a reading exercise where some of the words are missing and you must put them back in. Read the story below. Every eighth word has been taken out and is listed below the passage. Fill in the blanks with the words you think will make sense.

allowing	are	birds	can	from	in	inserted	living	narrow
nuts	of	on	or	parrot	sip	small	that	their

Bills are Tools

The bill of a bird can tell you a lot about what it eats and how it gets its food. The heron has a long pointed bill **that** looks like a spear. This bird wades **in** shallow water and spears passing fish. Some **birds** , like the spoonbill, have long bills that **are** flattened near the tip. They can use **their** odd shaped bill to shovel small fish **from** mud or water. The shorter pointed bill **of** the woodpecker is used like a chisel **or** drill. They poke small holes into trees, **allowing** the woodpecker to expose the tiny insects **living** under the bark. The sparrow and robin have **small** bills that act as tweezers. These birds **can** easily pick up seeds and insects found **on** the ground. The hummingbird has a long **narrow** bill, like a straw. The bill is **inserted** deep into a flower and used to **sip** nectar. A strong hooked bill, like the **parrot** has, is useful in cracking seeds and **nuts** with hard shells. Next time you are bird watching, see if you can figure out how the bird uses its bill.

©1995 Kelley Wingate Publications 69 KW 1018

Name _____ Skill: cloze

Cloze is a reading exercise where some of the words are missing and you must put them back in. Read the story below. Every eighth word has been taken out and is listed below the passage. Fill in the blanks with the words you think will make sense.

also	As	because	caves	deep	developed	fish	fish
food	have	most	spent	themselves	there	they	

Cave Fish

One of the strangest types of fish is called the cave fish. These fish have been found deep in **caves** all over the world. What makes this **fish** so strange is that it is blind. **As** a matter of fact, some cave fish **have** no eyes at all! These fish have **spent** their entire lives in pools or lakes **deep** under the ground. There is no light **there** , so even if the fish had eyes **they** would be of little use. The cave **fish** are far from helpless, however. They have **developed** keen senses of smell and touch so **food** can be found easily. These strong senses **also** enable the fish to avoid being caught **themselves.** These animals have pale, almost invisible skin **because** they lack the skin pigment necessary in **most** animals as protection from the sun. These fish are living examples of how animals can adapt to their environment.

©1995 Kelley Wingate Publications 70 KW 1018

Answer Key

Name _____
Skill: cloze

Cloze is a reading exercise where some of the words are missing and you must put them back in. Read the story below. Every eighth word has been taken out and is listed below the passage. Fill in the blanks with the words you think will make sense.

and	anything	arms	did	disappeared	done	feeling	He	he
inch	pile	skates	stepped	the	wanted	was	wet	

Hockey

A fresh snow had fallen during the night. Hal was busily shoveling the side of __the__ pond where the ice had frozen solid. __He__ lifted shovel after shovel of the heavy __wet__ snow and carried it over the the __pile__ he was making on the bank. Hal __did__ not like to shovel snow, but there __was__ no other way to get the job __done__. Before long the ice was cleared. Hal's __arms__ ached as he pulled off his boots __and__ slipped his feet into a pair of __skates__. He picked up his hockey stick and __stepped__ onto the cleared ice. Pain and fatigue __disappear__ as Hal glided across the smooth surface, __feeling__ the cold wind against his cheeks. Every __inch__ of his body came to life as __he__ guided the puck with his stick. Hal __wanted__ to be a hockey player more than __anything__ else in the world. This was his dream, and Hal was willing to do whatever might take to make that dream come true.

©1995 Kelley Wingate Publications   71   KW 1018

Name _____
Skill: cloze

Cloze is a reading exercise where some of the words are missing and you must put them back in. Read the story below. Every fifth word has been taken out and is listed below the passage. Fill in the blanks with the words you think will make sense.

a	a	all	at	because	family	have	hotel	I	In
My	national	near	other	part	picked	reads	so		
the	the	to	to	to	vacation	vote	what		

Family Vacation

It is a lot of fun to take a trip to new places. Planning the trip is __part__ of the excitement. My __family__ looks at maps and __reads__ books about different places. __In__ June we each pick __a__ place we would like __to__ go for our summer __vacation__. Then we tell each __other__ about the place we __have__ chosen. We talk about __the__ things we can do __at__ the place we have __picked__. Dad always chooses a __national__ park because he likes __to__ camp. Mom usually picks __a__ city with a nice __hotel__ and lots of museums. __My__ brother chooses a place __near__ a lake or river __because__ he likes to fish. __I__ change hobbies every year, __so__ you can never tell __what__ area I will select! When __the__ family has heard about __all__ the different places we __vote__ on where we want __to__ go. No matter what the decision is, we all agree that our vacations are a lot of fun.

©1995 Kelley Wingate Publications   72   KW 1018

Name _____
Skill: cloze

Cloze is a reading exercise where some of the words are missing and you must put them back in. Read the story below. Every fifth word has been taken out and is listed below the passage. Fill in the blanks with the words you think will make sense.

and	bent	compete	five	golf	hit	is	large	on	Players	playing
sand	Scottish	spread	to	use	wanted	what	where	with		

Golf

The Romans invented one sport called paganica that has developed into a popular sport today. The Roman emperors enjoyed __playing__ this game when they __wanted__ to relax. They would __use__ a bent stick to __hit__ a soft ball stuffed __with__ feathers. For the next __five__ hundred years the game __spread__ and was further developed __on__ several different continents. The __Scottish__ refined the game into __what__ we know today as __golf__. Today we use metal __and__ wooden clubs instead of __bent__ sticks. The course (place __where__ the game is played) __is__ usually filled with trees, __sand__ pits, and water holes __to__ make the game challenging. __Players__ from around the world __compete__ in this game for __large__ cash prizes. Although the game is not quite the same as the Romans played it, it is still a relaxing and fun sport.

©1995 Kelley Wingate Publications   73   KW 1018

Name _____
Skill: vocabulary

An affix is any letter or group of letters added to a word. If the affix is at the beginning of the word, it is a *prefix*. If it is added to the end of a word, it is a *suffix*. Below is a list of the most common affixes.

PREFIXES: ab- ad- be- com- de- dis- en- em- in- pre- pro- re- sub- un-
SUFFIXES: -ion -ition -ation -ful -less -ic -an -ian -y -ance -ant -ence -er -ness -ment -able -ible -en -ous -ure -ity -ly -ive -s -es -d -ed -ing

These affixes may be added to a root word to form another word. Listed below are four words to which an affix has been added. Identify the root word and write it on the first line. Then make five more words by adding a different affix.

A. comparable
root word __compare__   1. __comparable__
2. __compares__   3. __uncomparable__
4. __compared__   5. __comparison__

B. disorderly
root word __order__   1. __disorderly__
2. __disorder__   3. __reorder__
4. __orderly__   5. __ordering__

C. mistaken
root word __take__   1. __mistaken__
2. __retake__   3. __taker__
4. __taking__   5. __mistakenly__

D. talkative
root word __talk__   1. __untalkative__
2. __talkative__   3. __talks__
4. __talker__   5. __talking__

©1995 Kelley Wingate Publications   74   KW 1018

Answer Key

Page 75 (top left)

Name _____ Skill: vocabulary

An affix is any letter or group of letters added to a word. If the affix is at the beginning of the word, it is a *prefix*. If it is added to the end of a word, it is a *suffix*. Below is a list of the most common affixes.

PREFIXES: ab- ad- be- com- de- dis- en- em- in- pre- pro- re- sub- un-
SUFFIXES: -ion -ition -ation -ful -less -ic -an -ian -n -al -ary -y -ance -ant -ence -er -ness -ment -able -ible -en -ous -ure -ity -ly -ive -s -es -d -ed -ing

These affixes may be added to a root word to form another word. Listed below are four words to which an affix has been added. Identify the root word and write it on the first line. Then make five more words by adding a different affix.

A. recoil
   root word __coil__   1. __recoil__
   2. __recoiled__   3. __recoiling__
   4. __coiling__   5. __coiled__

B. unmoved
   root word __move__   1. __remove__
   2. __removed__   3. __mover__
   4. __moving__   5. __unmoved__

C. tingly
   root word __tingle__   1. __tingled__
   2. __tingles__   3. __tingling__
   4. __tingly__   5. __tinglable__

D. spinner
   root word __spin__   1. __respin__
   2. __spinners__   3. __spins__
   4. __spinning__   5. __respinning__

©1995 Kelley Wingate Publications   75   KW 1018

Page 76 (top right)

Name _____ Skill: vocabulary

An affix is any letter or group of letters added to a word. If the affix is at the beginning of the word, it is a *prefix*. If it is added to the end of a word, it is a *suffix*. Below is a list of the most common affixes.

PREFIXES: ab- ad- be- com- de- dis- en- em- in- pre- pro- re- sub- un-
SUFFIXES: -ion -ition -ation -ful -less -ic -an -ian -n -al -ary -y -ance -ant -ence -er -ness -ment -able -ible -en -ous -ure -ity -ly -ive -s -es -d -ed -ing

These affixes may be added to a root word to form another word. Listed below are four words to which an affix has been added. Identify the root word and write it on the first line. Then make five more words by adding a different affix.

A. repose
   root word __pose__   1. __poser__
   2. __composed__   3. __unposed__
   4. __posing__   5. __dispose__

B. passable
   root word __pass__   1. __unpassing__
   2. __passive__   3. __compassion__
   4. __passable__   5. __passed__

C. learner
   root word __learn__   1. __relearn__
   2. __learner__   3. __learning__
   4. __learned__   5. __learns__

D. dazedly
   root word __daze__   1. __undazed__
   2. __dazes__   3. __dazing__
   4. __dazed__   5. __dazled__

©1995 Kelley Wingate Publications   76   KW 1018

Page 77 (bottom left)

Name _____ Skill: vocabulary

An affix is any letter or group of letters added to a word. If the affix is at the beginning of the word, it is a *prefix*. If it is added to the end of a word, it is a *suffix*. Below is a list of the most common affixes.

PREFIXES: ab- ad- be- com- de- dis- en- em- in- pre- pro- re- sub- un-
SUFFIXES: -ion -ition -ation -ful -less -ic -an -ian -n -al -ary -y -ance -ant -ence -er -ness -ment -able -ible -en -ous -ure -ity -ly -ive -s -es -d -ed -ing

These affixes may be added to a root word to form another word. Listed below are four words to which an affix has been added. Identify the root word and write it on the first line. Then make five more words by adding a different affix.

A. amazingly
   root word __amaze__   1. __unamazed__
   2. __amazement__   3. __amazes__
   4. __unamazing__   5. __amazed__

B. clippings
   root word __clip__   1. __unclipped__
   2. __clipper__   3. __clipping__
   4. __clipped__   5. __clips__

C. electrified
   root word __electric__   1. __electrically__
   2. __electricity__   3. __electrition__
   4. __electrify__   5. __electrical__

D. mistreated
   root word __treat__   1. __retreat__
   2. __untreated__   3. __treating__
   4. __treats__   5. __treatment__

©1995 Kelley Wingate Publications   77   KW 1018

Page 78 (bottom right)

Name _____ Skill: vocabulary

An affix is any letter or group of letters added to a word. If the affix is at the beginning of the word, it is a *prefix*. If it is added to the end of a word, it is a *suffix*. Below is a list of the most common affixes.

PREFIXES: ab- ad- be- com- de- dis- en- em- in- pre- pro- re- sub- un-
SUFFIXES: -ion -ition -ation -ful -less -ic -an -ian -n -al -ary -y -ance -ant -ence -er -ness -ment -able -ible -en -ous -ure -ity -ly -ive -s -es -d -ed -ing

These affixes may be added to a root word to form another word. Listed below are four words to which an affix has been added. Identify the root word and write it on the first line. Then make five more words by adding a different affix.

A. specifically
   root word __specific__   1. __specify__
   2. __specifically__   3. __unspecific__
   4. __specified__   5. __specification__

B. preserver
   root word __preserve__   1. __preservation__
   2. __preserver__   3. __unpreserved__
   4. __preserves__   5. __preservable__

C. workings
   root word __work__   1. __unworkable__
   2. __worker__   3. __unworked__
   4. __rework__   5. __working__

D. uninteresting
   root word __interest__   1. __uninterested__
   2. __disinterested__   3. __interestingly__
   4. __interestable__   5. __interesting__

©1995 Kelley Wingate Publications   78   KW 1018

Answer Key

Name _____   Skill: vocabulary

An affix is any letter or group of letters added to a word. If the affix is at the beginning of the word, it is a *prefix*. If it is added to the end of a word, it is a *suffix*. Below is a list of the most common affixes.

PREFIXES: ab- ad- be- com- de- dis- en- em- in- pre- pro- re- sub- un-
SUFFIXES: -ion -ition -ation -ful -less -ic -an -ian -n -al -ary -y -ance -ant -ence -er -ness -ment -able -ible -en -ous -ure -ity -ly -ive -s -es -d -ed -ing

These affixes may be added to a root word to form another word. Listed below are four words to which an affix has been added. Identify the root word and write it on the first line. Then make five more words by adding a different affix.

A. thoughtless

root word thought   1. thoughtful
2. thoughtfully   3. thoughtfulness
4. rethought   5. thoughtlessly

B. productive

root word produce   1. unproductive
2. reproduce   3. productively
4. production   5. producing

C. insanity

root word sane   1. insane
2. sanely   3. sanity
4. saneness   5. sanitary

D. flatness

root word flat   1. unflattened
2. flatten   3. reflatten
4. flatter   5. flatly

©1995 Kelley Wingate Publications   79   KW 1018

Name _____   Skill: vocabulary

An affix is any letter or group of letters added to a word. If the affix is at the beginning of the word, it is a *prefix*. If it is added to the end of a word, it is a *suffix*. Below is a list of the most common affixes.

PREFIXES: ab- ad- be- com- de- dis- en- em- in- pre- pro- re- sub- un-
SUFFIXES: -ion -ition -ation -ful -less -ic -an -ian -n -al -ary -y -ance -ant -ence -er -ness -ment -able -ible -en -ous -ure -ity -ly -ive -s -es -d -ed -ing

These affixes may be added to a root word to form another word. Listed below are four words to which an affix has been added. Identify the root word and write it on the first line. Then make five more words by adding a different affix.

A. earnings

root word earn   1. unearned
2. earned   3. earning
4. earner   5. earnest

B. freshened

root word fresh   1. freshener
2. refresh   3. unfresh
4. freshen   5. freshness

C. fruitful

root word fruit   1. unfruitful
2. fruity   3. fruiter
4. fruitfully   5. fruition

D. decidedly

root word decide   1. undecided
2. decidable   3. decidedness
4. deciding   5. deciduous

©1995 Kelley Wingate Publications   80   KW 1018

Name _____   Skill: vocabulary

An affix is any letter or group of letters added to a word. If the affix is at the beginning of the word, it is a *prefix*. If it is added to the end of a word, it is a *suffix*. Below is a list of the most common affixes.

PREFIXES: ab- ad- be- com- de- dis- en- em- in- pre- pro- re- sub- un-
SUFFIXES: -ion -ition -ation -ful -less -ic -an -ian -n -al -ary -y -ance -ant -ence -er -ness -ment -able -ible -en -ous -ure -ity -ly -ive -s -es -d -ed -ing

These affixes may be added to a root word to form another word. Listed below are four words to which an affix has been added. Identify the root word and write it on the first line. Then make five more words by adding a different affix.

A. disconnect

root word connect   1. connective
2. connecter   3. unconneted
4. reconnecting   5. connection

B. assumed

root word assume   1. unassuming
2. assumable   3. assuming
4. assumedly   5. assumption

C. disheartened

root word heart   1. heartily
2. heartiness   3. heartless
4. hearty   5. hearten

D. exceeding

root word exceed   1. unexceeded
2. exceedingly   3. exceeded
4. exceeds   5. unexceeding

©1995 Kelley Wingate Publications   81   KW 1018

Name _____   Skill: vocabulary

An affix is any letter or group of letters added to a word. If the affix is at the beginning of the word, it is a *prefix*. If it is added to the end of a word, it is a *suffix*. Below is a list of the most common affixes.

PREFIXES: ab- ad- be- com- de- dis- en- em- in- pre- pro- re- sub- un-
SUFFIXES: -ion -ition -ation -ful -less -ic -an -ian -n -al -ary -y -ance -ant -ence -er -ness -ment -able -ible -en -ous -ure -ity -ly -ive -s -es -d -ed -ing

These affixes may be added to a root word to form another word. Listed below are four words to which an affix has been added. Identify the root word and write it on the first line. Then make five more words by adding a different affix.

A. laughable

root word laugh   1. unlaughing
2. laughingly   3. laughless
4. laugher   5. laughed

B. recollect

root word collect   1. colletion
2. collected   3. collectively
4. collectivism   5. collectable

C. wizened

root word wise   1. unwise
2. wizard   3. wiser
4. wisest   5. wisely

D. typist

root word type   1. retype
2. typify   3. typed
4. typing   5. typical

©1995 Kelley Wingate Publications   82   KW 1018

Answer Key

Page 83

Name _____   Skill: vocabulary

An affix is any letter or group of letters added to a word. If the affix is at the beginning of the word, it is a *prefix*. If it is added to the end of a word, it is a *suffix*. Below is a list of the most common affixes.

PREFIXES: ab- ad- be- com- de- dis- en- em- in- pre- pro- re- sub- un-
SUFFIXES: -ion -ition -ation -ful -less -ic -an -ian -n -al -ary -y -ance -ant -ence -er -ness -ment -able -ible -en -ous -ure -ity -ly -ive -s -es -d -ed -ing

These affixes may be added to a root word to form another word. Listed below are four words to which an affix has been added. Identify the root word and write it on the first line. Then make five more words by adding a different affix.

A. stopper
root word **stop**   1. **unstoppable**
2. **unstopped**   3. **stops**
4. **stopple**   5. **stoppage**

B. shelved
root word **shelve**   1. **reshelve**
2. **unshelve**   3. **shelving**
4. **disheveled**   5. **shelving**

C. paring
root word **pare**   1. **prepare**
2. **pared**   3. **unprepared**
4. **preparing**   5. **compare**

D. mockingly
root word **Mock**   1. **unmocking**
2. **Mocked**   3. **mockery**
4. **mocking**   5. **Mocks**

©1995 Kelley Wingate Publications   83   KW 1018

Page 84

1. **Read each word below and write the first definition that comes to mind.**

charge **credit**   counter **shelf**
chief **important leader**   crook **thief**
coast **shoreline**   cross **crucifix**
complete **finish**   current **new or latest**

2. **These same words have been used in the sentences below. Write a definition for each word as it is used in the sentence. Compare the definition with your first choice.**

1. The elephants began to **charge** when they heard the guns.
2. The **chief** reason we are doing the report is because we like the subject.
3. Sally stopped pedaling the bicycle and began to **coast** down the hill.
4. I have a **complete** set of baseball cards.
5. I will **counter** your idea with a new one.
6. The bird built its nest in a **crook** on the bottom limb of the tree.
7. Aunt Sara was **cross** because we broke her window.
8. An electrical **current** runs through that wire so be very careful.

3. **Give a definition for the word as it is used in the sentence.**

charge **run at; attack**
chief **main**
coast **move without effort**
complete **total; all**
counter **oppose**
crook **bend or curve**
cross **angry**
current **flow or stream**

©1995 Kelley Wingate Publications   84   KW 1018

Page 85

1. **Read each word below and write the first definition that comes to mind.**

draft **cold air or wind**   fair **equal**
spell **call out letters**   fashion **clothing style**
drop **let fall**   flag **a banner**
express **fast**   fudge **kind of chocolate**

2. **These same words have been used in the sentences below. Write a definition for each word as it is used in the sentence. Compare the definition with your first choice.**

1. This first copy of my paper is only the rough **draft.**
2. I am very tired and need to just sit down for a **spell.**
3. Did I just feel a **drop** of rain?
4. Do you have an **express** flight to New York?
5. The child had **fair** skin and blue eyes.
6. Joan can **fashion** a vase out of old milk bottles.
7. John began to **flag** after running only one mile. He was too tired to finish the race.
8. No one is allowed to **fudge** on this test. If you are caught you will fail it!

3. **Give a definition for the word as it is used in the sentence.**

draft **unfinished product**
spell **a short while**
drop **a spot of water**
express **no stop**
fair **light or pale**
fashion **make or mold**
flag **tire**
fudge **cheat**

©1995 Kelley Wingate Publications   85   KW 1018

Page 86

1. **Read each word below and write the first definition that comes to mind.**

litter **trash**   sand **gritty material**
long **not short**   season **winter, spring, etc...**
produce **make**   sharp **pointed**
resort **spa**   staple **a fastener**

2. **These same words have been used in the sentences below. Write a definition for each word as it is used in the sentence. Compare the definition with your first choice.**

1. Our dog just had a **litter** of puppies.
2. I **long** for a cold glass of water because I am so hot and thirsty.
3. You will find fruits and vegetables in the **produce** department at the grocery store.
4. Please do not **resort** to calling me names.
5. **Sand** the wood before you paint it.
6. **Season** the meat with salt before you eat it.
7. Eric is a very **sharp** student. He always gets great grades!
8. Bread is a **staple** food in our house. We have it at every meal.

3. **Give a definition for the word as it is used in the sentence.**

litter **group**
long **desire**
produce **fruits and vegetables**
resort **a source of help**
sand **smooth by grinding**
season **salt or pepper, use herbs**
sharp **smart**
staple **basic**

©1995 Kelley Wingate Publications   86   KW 1018

©1995 Kelley Wingate Publications   123   CD-3715

Answer Key

Worksheet (page 87)

Name _____   Skill: vocabulary

1. Read each word below and write the first definition that comes to mind.

tense	uptight, nervous	raise	lift up
toast	browned bread	stage	a raised platform
troop	a group of people	steer	drive, guide
type	push keys with fingers	stalk	stem

2. These same words have been used in the sentences below. Write a definition for each word as it is used in the sentence. Compare the definition with your first choice.

1. Make sure that you use the proper **tense** of the verb.
2. The best man will make the **toast** at the wedding.
3. The class will **troop** to library after lunch.
4. A glass is a **type** of container for water.
5. I don't think I ever want to **raise** children!
6. The first **stage** of the plan is to brainstorm for new ideas.
7. That **steer** with the long horns will be perfect for the rodeo.
8. The thief would **stalk** his victims by following them in his car.

3. Give a definition for the word as it is used in the sentence.

tense   form of a verb
toast   speech in honor of someone
troop   move in a crowd
type   kind
raise   rear; bring up
stage   step in a process
steer   male cow
stalk   search for or follow

©1995 Kelley Wingate Publications   87   KW 1018

Worksheet (page 88)

Name _____   Skill: vocabulary

1. Read each word below and write the first definition that comes to mind.

stem	trunk of a plant	bridge	a span across a river
stern	harsh	brush	to comb hair
scrap	a small bit	curry	a spice
bluff	fool	drove	past tense of drive

2. These same words have been used in the sentences below. Write a definition for each word as it is used in the sentence. Compare the definition with your first choice.

1. We must **stem** this problem before it gets any worse.
2. A flag usually hangs on the **stern** on a ship.
3. Karen got into a **scrap** with her best friend.
4. The artist liked to sit on a **bluff** high above the ocean.
5. My parents like to play **bridge** every Wednesday night.
6. The hunters sat in the **brush** four hours before they saw a deer.
7. You must **curry** the horse with a large brush before you put it in the stall.
8. A **drove** of cattle was crossing the road so we had to stop and wait for them.

3. Give a definition for the word as it is used in the sentence.

stem   stop
stern   back of a boat
scrap   a fight
bluff   high cliff
bridge   a card game
brush   bushes
curry   comb or brush
drove   herd

©1995 Kelley Wingate Publications   88   KW 1018

Worksheet (page 89)

Name _____   Skill: vocabulary

1. Read each word below and write the first definition that comes to mind.

entrance	way in	fold	double over
fawn	young deer	fresh	not stale
fell	past tense of fall	fuse	a wick
firm	hard or solid	stall	hesitate; horse pen

2. These same words have been used in the sentences below. Write a definition for each word as it is used in the sentence. Compare the definition with your first choice.

1. The sound of bagpipes can **entrance** many people.
2. I cannot stand it when you **fawn** over me because you want a favor.
3. The villain sneered before he did his **fell** deed.
4. My mother works for a law **firm**.
5. The sheep were in the **fold** for the night.
6. The young child was being **fresh** with his mother so she sent him to his room.
7. We will **fuse** the pieces together so they will not come apart again.
8. The vendor set up his **stall** at the fair so he could sell his goods.

3. Give a definition for the word as it is used in the sentence.

entrance   delight
fawn   overly affectionate
fell   evil; awful
firm   company
fold   a pen
fresh   sassy
fuse   bond together
stall   booth

©1995 Kelley Wingate Publications   89   KW 1018

Worksheet (page 90)

Name _____   Skill: vocabulary

1. Read each word below and write the first definition that comes to mind.

grave	hole in the ground	hold	hang on to
hamper	clothes basket	incense	burned perfume
hawk	a bird	jerky	dumb
heel	bottom of foot	jet	type of plane

2. These same words have been used in the sentences below. Write a definition for each word as it is used in the sentence. Compare the definition with your first choice.

1. This is a very **grave** matter, and you should not laugh about it.
2. That coat is too long and will **hamper** you when you run.
3. The popcorn vendor began to **hawk** his goods at the circus.
4. The sailboat began to **heel** as the wind blew harder.
5. Sailors store cargo in the **hold** of the ship.
6. Your rude comments **incense** me.
7. Many cowboys ate **jerky** because it would not spoil during long cattle drives.
8. We used a **jet** of air to blow the leaves from the lawn.

3. Give a definition for the word as it is used in the sentence.

grave   serious
hamper   impede; get in the way
hawk   sell
heel   tip over
hold   storage area
incense   make angry
jerky   dried meat
jet   stream

©1995 Kelley Wingate Publications   90   KW 1018

Answer Key

Name _____ Skill: vocabulary

1. Read each word below and write the first definition that comes to mind.

key _opener of a lock_   leave _go away_
lap _thighs when seated_   line _distance between two points._
lark _bird_   list _a group of items._
leagues _groups_   meter _a measurement_

2. These same words have been used in the sentences below. Write a definition for each word as it is used in the sentence. Compare the definition with your first choice.

1. The third **key** on the piano is broken.
2. Dogs and cats **lap** water to get a drink.
3. The boys put salt in the sugar bowl just for a **lark**.
4. Submarines can go many **leagues** under the ocean.
5. I give you my **leave** to go to the park with your friends.
6. I will **line** your jacket with flannel so it will be warmer.
7. The ship began to **list** when water poured in through the crack in the side.
8. We needed a new water **meter** so we could measure how much we used each month.

3. Give a definition for the word as it is used in the sentence.

key _lever used to produce music_
lap _to drink using the tongue_
lark _prank; frolic_
leagues _a measurement_
leave _permission_
line _cover an inner surface_
list _tip to one side_
meter _instrument to measure usage_

Name _____ Skill: vocabulary

1. Read each word below and write the first definition that comes to mind.

nip _bite_   press _iron_
pitch _throw_   quack _sound a duck makes_
pine _type of tree_   refuse _to say no_
post _a support_   rifle _type of gun_

2. These same words have been used in the sentences below. Write a definition for each word as it is used in the sentence. Compare the definition with your first choice.

1. I would like just a **nip** from your bottle of soda.
2. The workers filled the holes in the road with **pitch**.
3. The puppy began to **pine** for its mother as soon as we took it out of the litter.
4. The guard could not leave his **post** even for a minute.
5. The **press** reported on the hurricane that was headed our way.
6. That doctor is nothing but a **quack**.
7. The garbage collector put the **refuse** in the back of his truck.
8. Joe had to **rifle** through a stack of pictures before he found the one he wanted.

3. Give a definition for the word as it is used in the sentence.

nip _small sip_
pitch _tar_
pine _yearn for sadly_
post _a station_
press _news media_
quack _pretend doctor_
refuse _trash_
rifle _look through, search_

Name _____ Skill: vocabulary

1. Read each word below and write the first definition that comes to mind.

shed _small building_   snarl _growl_
shock _upset, jar_   soil _dirt_
shore _coastline_   strain _sift_
size _bigness, measure_   tart _sour_

2. These same words have been used in the sentences below. Write a definition for each word as it is used in the sentence. Compare the definition with your first choice.

1. **Shed** those wet clothes before you catch a cold!
2. The child had a **shock** of red hair and freckles.
3. We need to **shore** this porch before it falls down. See how it leans over there?
4. Please **size** this strip of wallpaper so we can hang it.
5. I have quite a **snarl** in my hair.
6. Do not **soil** your your best clothes by playing in the mud.
7. There is a new **strain** of the flu going around this year.
8. My grandmother baked a strawberry **tart** for dessert.

3. Give a definition for the word as it is used in the sentence.

shed _take off_
shock _bushy clump_
shore _support_
size _paste_
snarl _tangle_
soil _get dirty_
strain _kind or sort_
tart _pie_

Name _____ Skill: vocabulary

Read the following sentences. Use the context clues to help you decide what the word in boldface means. Circle the definition that you think best fits the word.

Example: We must **abolish** weapons in schools.
    permit   (ban)   allow

1. Garages are usually **adjacent** to houses.
    inside   (next to)   over

2. The empty building was **ablaze** by the time the fire trucks got there.
    full   (on fire)   torn down

3. I want to **amend** my last answer on that test. I have more to add to it.
    erase   turn in   (improve)

4. Joshua certainly has the **aptitude** for painting. He took first place at the show.
    (ability)   desire   quickness

5. I want to **assert** my opinion about the candidate.
    anchor   ban   (declare)

6. You will need to change your **attire** to dine there. They don't allow jeans.
    (manner of dress)   manner of eating   manner of writing

7. The designer made a **blueprint** of how the room will look when it is finished.
    color   photograph   (plan)

8. Joey is a **brawny** lad, which makes him great at football.
    decent   (muscular)   thin

9. Matt got his **breeches** wet when he sat too near the pool.
    books   shoes   (trousers)

10. I will **wager** that Mark wins the race!
    (bet)   brag   consider

Answer Key

Name _____ Skill: vocabulary

Read the following sentences. Use the context clues to help you decide what the word in boldface means. Circle the definition that you think best fits the word.

Example: We must **abolish** weapons in schools.
permit   (ban)   allow

1. Susan is **brusque** when she says what she thinks. She doesn't pull any punches!
   (blunt)   gentle   kind

2. The thieves found a **cache** for the stolen jewels.
   cash   (hiding place)   pocket

3. I don't mean to be **callous**, but I find it hard to feel sorry for you.
   funny   kind   (unfeeling)

4. That **canine** is barking and growling at us!
   blister   cat   (dog)

5. My legs were **chafed** after riding the horse all day.
   longer   (rubbed until sore)   tired out

6. Larry's mother really **chided** him for missing the school bus this morning.
   helped   laughed at   (scolded)

7. I don't understand this book. Can you **clarify** a few points for me?
   aide   help with   (make clear)

8. Helen is a **competent** worker, completing her work carefully.
   (capable)   confident   likely

9. I will **concede** to your wishes this time, but next time I get to choose.
   deny   fall   (grant)

10. The collar began to **constrict** around Danny's throat, making it hard to breathe.
    open   (squeeze)   tempt

Name _____ Skill: vocabulary

Read the following sentences. Use the context clues to help you decide what the word in boldface means. Circle the definition that you think best fits the word.

Example: We must **abolish** weapons in schools.
permit   (ban)   allow

1. You need a softer **contour** to that circle. The line is much too straight.
   color   mixture   (shape)

2. The puppy **cowered** in the corner when his master yelled at him.
   sat up   snuggled into   (shrunk from fear)

3. You are **daft** for suggesting that I drive. I haven't gotten a license yet!
   (foolish)   happy   honest

4. I **deem** it necessary to leave the party now.
   celebrate   fear   (think)

5. Judy must **despise** that movie. She said no one should go see it.
   adore   (hate)   love

6. The hunter pulled a **dirk** from its sheath and quickly cut the rope.
   (dagger)   can opener   tool

7. Help me **dismantle** this table so it will fit through the door.
   break   put together   (take apart)

8. The nurse **dispensed** the medicine to the patients.
   (gave out)   held   shot

9. Gloria was **elated** to hear she won the math contest.
   filled with fear   (filled with joy)   sad

10. The waves **eroded** the beach until the sand was nearly gone.
    filled up   splashed   (wore away)

Name _____ Skill: vocabulary

Read the following sentences. Use the context clues to help you decide what the word in boldface means. Circle the definition that you think best fits the word.

Example: We must **abolish** weapons in schools.
permit   (ban)   allow

1. That song always **evokes** tears when I hear it.
   brushes away   (calls forth)   washes

2. You are very smart and will **excel** in your studies if you try.
   (do very well)   fail   lag

3. What is for dinner? I am **famished**.
   in a hurry   (starving)   tired

4. The **flora** in the woods is always so green and lush this time of year.
   animals   growing   (plants)

5. I think I **fractured** my arm when I fell. Please call a doctor.
   (broke)   bruised   bumped

6. Beth acts so **giddy** when she wears a costume. It makes me laugh to watch her.
   grown up   serious   (silly)

7. I can't believe you **goaded** me into doing this when I didn't want to!
   asked   scared   (urged)

8. I prefer to live in a **hamlet** rather than a big city.
   country   house   (small village)

9. A **horde** of bees flew from the nest when Peg hit it with a stick.
   (swarm)   thick   vast distance

10. Teresa is in a **festive** mood this evening. I think she likes this party.
    dull   serious   (joyous)

Name _____ Skill: vocabulary

Read the following sentences. Use the context clues to help you decide what the word in boldface means. Circle the definition that you think best fits the word.

Example: We must **abolish** weapons in schools.
permit   (ban)   allow

1. You are so smart, it is hard to believe you could make such an **idiotic** statement!
   brilliant   (foolish)   quiet

2. This water is **impure** and not fit to drink.
   clear   cold   (not pure)

3. The boy stumbled near the puddle so much it was **inevitable** that he would fall in.
   (bound to happen)   not likely   radiant

4. The small mound of dirt was **infested** with ants.
   nearly empty   (swarming)   wasted

5. I will **inquire** about the departure time for the plane.
   (ask)   fumble   require

6. It is a miracle that the vase is still **intact** after falling on this hard floor.
   broken   guarded   (undamaged)

7. The sailor turned off the motor and put up the **jib** because the wind began to blow.
   anchor   rope   (sail)

8. Water dripped from the dog's **jowls** after he drank thirstily.
   (lower jaw)   paws   tail

9. I need to more flour to make this bread. Please get a sack from the **larder** in the kitchen.
   back yard   cellar   (pantry)

10. Please write your assignment in a **legible** manner so I won't need and interpreter to understand it.
    design   (readable)   thoughtless

Answer Key

Name _____   Skill: vocabulary

Read the following sentences. Use the context clues to help you decide what the word in boldface means. Circle the definition that you think best fits the word.

Example: We must **abolish** weapons in schools.
permit   (ban)   allow

1. Don't play with that chemical because swallowing it is **lethal**.
   (deadly)   legal   warm

2. The thought that it will rain on this beautiful sunny day is **ludicrous**.
   happy   (ridiculous)   smart

3. The children made a **valiant** effort to clean up that big empty lot, but the job was was too big.
   (brave)   gentle   timid

4. If those two companies **merge** they will become the biggest company in the state.
   back down   part ways   (unite)

5. The room was filled with the **mirth** of young children during the party.
   boots   (joy)   sleepiness

6. Joyce's face was **mottled** when she had the measles.
   creased and wrinkled   (marked with spots)   tightly drawn

7. The **wayfarer** looked as if he had come a great distance with that heavy suitcase.
   cab driver   father   (traveler)

8. Using gum instead of glue is a **novel** idea!
   fancy   patterned   (unusual)

9. That sun bonnet is terribly **outmoded**. Find a better hat to wear.
   dry   (old fashioned)   pretty

10. I am **parched**. Could I please have a big glass of water?
    angry   starving   (very dry)

©1995 Kelley Wingate Publications   99   KW 1018

Name _____   Skill: vocabulary

Read the following sentences. Use the context clues to help you decide what the word in boldface means. Circle the definition that you think best fits the word.

Example: We must **abolish** weapons in schools.
permit   (ban)   allow

1. Those flowers will **perish** if you don't put them in water right away.
   bloom   (die or spoil)   wander

2. The student looked **perplexed** when the teacher spoke in another language.
   happy   nervous   (puzzled)

3. You can **preserve** your drawing by putting it in a frame with glass.
   (keep or save)   sketch   watch

4. The **primary** reason for going to school is to learn.
   easiest   (first or most important)   least likely

5. The broken glass in the road **punctured** the tire.
   blasted   jacked up   (made a hole in)

6. I will **rebel** if you tell me I have to wash the dishes again tonight.
   (disobey)   go back to bed   love the idea

7. Sandy **recoiled** when his hand accidentally brushed against the snake.
   considered   (drew back)   grabbed

8. I can **recollect** a time when bread cost only ten cents a loaf!
   make up   look at   (remember)

9. James would like to **reform** our plan a little. He has some really good ideas to improve it.
   (change)   cushion   try it out

10. The smell of that skunk is enough to **repel** even a person with a stuffy nose!
    attract   (drive away)   odor

©1995 Kelley Wingate Publications   100   KW 1018

Name _____   Skill: vocabulary

Read the following sentences. Use the context clues to help you decide what the word in boldface means. Circle the definition that you think best fits the word.

Example: We must **abolish** weapons in schools.
permit   (ban)   allow

1. I am tired and need to **repose** myself.
   fan   (rest)   stand up

2. You have been working for hours. It is time for a **respite**.
   bicycle ride   piece of cake   (short rest)

3. We will **revere** the memory of this great person for the rest of our lives.
   attack   forget   (honor)

4. We were **scantily** equipped for such a long trip. We quickly ran out of food.
   (barely enough)   heavily   well

5. The man was gritting his teeth and his face was dark looking. It was easy to see that he was **seething** about something.
   (angry)   choking   elated

6. I wondered how the baby could sleep so **serenely** in the middle of the storm.
   in a ball   noisily   (peacefully)

7. This diamond you bought is a worthless **sham**.
   (fake)   jewel   shape

8. Mike polished his shoes until they had quite a **sheen** on them.
   dark look   shoelace   (shine)

9. The boys took the **skiff** across the lake this morning.
   kite   small animal   (small boat)

10. Erin was **sopping** after she stood in the rain for an hour.
    very cold   very dry   (very wet)

©1995 Kelley Wingate Publications   101   KW 1018

Name _____   Skill: vocabulary

Read the following sentences. Use the context clues to help you decide what the word in boldface means. Circle the definition that you think best fits the word.

Example: We must **abolish** weapons in schools.
permit   (ban)   allow

1. My baby grand piano will fit well in this **spacious** apartment.
   lovely   (roomy)   well lit

2. Rita showed a lot of **spunk** when she stood up to that bully.
   (courage)   fear   silliness

3. The rotting onion created a terrible **stench** in the refrigerator.
   fragrance   stain   (stink)

4. I think two sandwiches each should **suffice**.
   (be enough)   direct   make hungry

5. The tramp wore **tattered** clothes and there were holes in his shoes.
   (ragged)   tidy   trim

6. My mother tends to be **testy** when she has a headache.
   available   (cranky)   mellow

7. Everyone is wearing that kind of shoe these days. It must be a new **trend**.
   (current style)   development   sneaker

8. The dog had an **uncanny** way of knowing when I was on my way home.
   bent   keen   (weird)

9. The traveler had not washed or shaved in days, and his clothes were **unkempt**.
   clean   (not neat)   soggy

10. Don't worry about losing the game. It is a **trivial** matter.
    lasting   (unimportant)   very important

©1995 Kelley Wingate Publications   102   KW 1018

Reading Award

_____

receives this award for

_____

Keep up the great work!

_____   _____

signed   date

Reading Award

_____

receives this award for

_____

Great Job!

Great Job!

_____   _____

signed   date

                                    CD-3715

You Did It!

earns this award for

_____

Keep Up The Great Work!

_____   _____
Signed   Date

Certificate of Completion

This certificate certifies that

_____

Has completed

_____

Signed _____

Date _____

Great Success!

_____ earns this award for

_____

I am Proud of You!

_____
Signed

_____
Date

Congratulations!

Receives this award for

_____

Keep up the great work!

_____

Signed

_____

Date

Great Job!

Receives this award for

_____

Keep up the great work!

_____

Signed

_____

Date

Keep up the Great Work!

_____ earns this award for

_____

You are TERRIFIC!

Signed _____

Date _____

astronaut	again	address	about
beginning	basketball	baseball	autumn
buy	bottom	birthday	best
capital	candy	camel	cactus

chest	chase	catcher	careful
cross	crater	crack	classroom
dinner	detail	desk	darkness
easy	early	during	dock

favorite	excite	envelope	end
garden	front	friend	fireman
head	hamburger	hair	great
late	kisses	hungry	homework

main	ocean	period	present
lunch	month	path	pour
lightening	money	party	pool
leash	middle	order	pick

reason	rather	race	quiet
sent	seed	scary	rinse
smell	skunk	shower	shopping
storm	stood	spring	spray

strange	street	student	sunlight
table	terrible	thunder	toast
total	visit	water	wishbone
wonderful	write	web	wisk